PENG

ME AND MA

Divya Dutta is an Indian actress who has worked in over eighty feature films. She was born and raised in Ludhiana, Punjab. She has established a successful career in Bollywood and Punjabi cinema, and has also appeared in other Indian-language and international productions. She is noted for playing a wide variety of roles in different genres, and is one of the leading actresses of parallel cinema. Dutta has won several awards and recognitions in the film industry including the IIFA and Zee Cine best supporting actress awards.

Me&Ma

CELEBRATING ZINDAGI...

DIVYA DUTTA

PENGUIN BOOKS

PENGUIN BOOKS

USA | Canada | UK | Ireland | Australia
New Zealand | India | South Africa | China

Penguin Books is part of the Penguin Random House group of companies
whose addresses can be found at global.penguinrandomhouse.com

Published by Penguin Random House India Pvt. Ltd
7th Floor, Infinity Tower C, DLF Cyber City,
Gurgaon 122 002, Haryana, India

First published in Penguin Books by Penguin Random House India 2017

ISBN 9780143426790

Typeset in Garamond Premier Pro by Manipal Digital Systems, Manipal
Printed at Thomson Press India Ltd, New Delhi

www.penguin.co.in

Contents

❦

Foreword

Not without My Daughter

⌒

They were inseparable; I could never imagine Divya without her. I always saw them together not because she had nothing to do but because mother and daughter enjoyed spending time with each other more than with anyone else. She was interested in literature and poetry and life. I had the privilege of meeting her on different sets and we spent time chatting about various matters. Nalini Dutta was different from what a first glance at her would suggest.

When I read Divya's account of her, I realized how different her life had been. Widowed early in life, she became both mother and father to her two children. Her zest for life, her spirit of adventure cheered them on. At the age of nineteen, when

Divya got a proposal from a well-settled doctor in the USA, her nani and uncle were keen to not let go of what they considered 'a good catch'. Then came a resolute 'no' from Naliniji. 'My daughter is too young to marry right now. I want to give her some time . . .' And she did. She supported her daughter through thick and thin to nurture her every desire, to fulfil her every dream steadfastly, through all the ups and downs life offered them.

No wonder her daughter Divya depended so much on her—for guidance, for love, for security. She taught her children the values of integrity, commitment and professional ethics. Having been a doctor, and having practised under less than ideal surroundings, she had learnt that one must give one's best, never mind the circumstances. The children learned from their mother almost by a process of osmosis. She exemplified all she believed in. She was Divya's pillar of strength, her life support. The book is replete with little vignettes, beautiful moments indented in the daughter's memories.

There is an incident in Delhi where the feisty mother whilst arguing with a boatman, falls into a pond! The ten-year-old Divya watches in panic and instead of bawling her heart out like children are wont to do, unmindful of the danger, jumps in to save her! I can hardly imagine any other young child reacting like that. It was as though the umbilical cord between them had never been severed ...

All too soon, however, the tables turned—inevitably. Naliniji's health started failing and in spite of being a doctor herself, she was unmindful of the toll it was taking on her. It fell on the children's lot to become caregivers for their mother. Rahul is a doctor himself and was vigilant in ensuring she was taking her medication on time, but Divya started treating her like one would an errant child, much to her mother's chagrin.

Siblings always take on one of either roles—good cop, bad cop—and in Naliniji's view, Divya was certainly the bad cop! She did know in her heart that the roles had reversed. The daughter was becoming the mother. Life was turning full circle.

Anyone who has been a caregiver for an ailing elder feels strong and helpless in turn and learns to take one day at a time ...

We were shooting for *Chalk and Duster* when I learned Naliniji's condition was worsening. True professional that she is, Divya continued to report on time and complete her work before she rushed back to the hospital. Each day, when she reported on the set, I didn't even need to ask how her mother was—I could clearly see it mirrored on her face. Hope as well as despair.

The end came soon after. When Javed and I went to pay our respects, Divya sat stoically, almost calmly. The tears had dried up. I knew then that the dam would need to burst at some time and till then it would be very difficult for her.

In the book, Divya writes of those difficult times with candour and heart-rending simplicity. I was left sobbing.

I'm very glad she decided to write this book. It will help her come to terms with denial, grief, despair, loneliness. Finally, in the book Divya ends with hope and strength, firm in the knowledge that her mother will always be with her.

I remember Anees Jung's letter to me after my father passed away: 'One never really loses a parent because in death, their soul, trapped in a frail body is set free and surrounds you like the air you breathe ...'

They will remain inseparable. I need not imagine Divya without Naliniji because she lives on in every breath her daughter takes.

Shabana Azmi

Author's Note

〜

It was a hot Monday afternoon and my car stopped at the entrance of a plush Juhu building. It was the office of one of the most renowned directors of the film industry. I entered the office and a bunch of people got up to greet me. It felt nice to see their smiling faces. I could feel that they were fond of me. I could feel that somewhere they acknowledged and appreciated my journey thus far and their getting up was a mark of respect for that.

The Indian film industry is huge. In spite of its vastness, everyone who is a part of it knows about the goings-on in the industry. Even if they don't talk about it openly, they are aware of each other's works and career trajectories.

Acknowledging everyone, I sat down to hear the role which was to be narrated by the director.

I heard the story in absolute silence. After he was done, he said, 'So we needed a strong woman for this role and who better than you . . .'

A smile appeared on my face. I wondered, when and how had I got this image? When and how had I become this strong? I used to be a timid child. Always safe in the shadows of my parents. I had always hidden behind Ma's pallu. What had given me the strength to walk my own path?

And then it struck me. It was Ma. She was the one who had held my hand as I'd walked this difficult path, trying to find my space in this industry. And as time rolled by, her presence had impacted me so much that I had drawn a lot of her into me. She was someone whose life had inspired me so much that I strived to be like her and somewhere, along the way, I'd become a mirror image of her.

My mother, my soulmate.

As I sit today penning my thoughts, sharing them with you, pouring out all that I feel, I write straight from my heart about my journey as a daughter and as a mother.

Yes, after a point of time there was a reversal of roles. I had become a Ma to my mother in the past few years, pampering her, scolding her for exactly the reasons I got scolded for as a child, holding her hand, taking her out for ice creams, outings, her favourite things to do. And yes, like any other mother–daughter duo we fought too, and she had her regular corner to go and sulk in, that, too, with an attitude! She knew I would go to her to make peace in exactly ten minutes, which I did. I just couldn't bear the thought of Ma being angry. That too with me. So after a whole lot of apologies and pampering, she would eventually give in. We would be best friends again and be nicely gossiping and chatting like nothing had happened, once again fussing over who would get the remote and get to see their favourite TV shows. Ninety-nine per cent of the time, Ma always won and we ended up watching the Zindagi channel!

She was a pillar of strength in trying times but she also did not forget to have fun with life. What she gave me was priceless—a beautiful journey— the memorable and cherished experiences and lessons which I put into my roles and my relationships with all my heart.

So dear reader, I share here all those integral moments of my life, which have made me who I am today and have taught me to face the storms of life head-on, without allowing the fear raging inside to surface. Ma taught me to overcome my fears and I drew my confidence from the knowledge of her presence. If anything went wrong and I had to look for support, she was there.

And even though she's not physically present today, I know she's still there with me. Standing right next to me.

Trying to come to terms with her absence in her physical form is an internal battle I have been fighting. I sometimes try to erase the past one year of my life from memory in order to not let go of her. Yet the events of the year keep flashing in front of my eyes every now and then, like a long bad dream. And I know Ma tries to make them go away and distract me with other thoughts. I know she wants me to only remember her happily. That's what she had always given me. Happiness.

And that's exactly what I am going to do through the pages of this book. Celebrate her and my life with her with all of you, a lifetime spent with a beautiful woman who I was fortunate to call Ma . . .

1

Down Memory Lane

I sat in the ICU holding her hand...

They had given us just a few more hours...

Just a few more hours of that beautiful journey with her...

She was unconscious and I sat there, numb.

Maybe it was all a bad dream.

Maybe it would all be fine.

Maybe we would both walk out of the ICU happily, hand in hand.

Her hand lay still on the side of the bed.

I got up and took my place beside her.

My head was on her arm and her hand firmly in mine.

I sang her favourite songs from Dilip Kumar films and recited poetry she had composed...

I had done this many times earlier. Today was different.

I was sure, though her eyes were shut, she could hear my every word . . .

There was so much to share in those few hours . . .

So much!

My entire life flashed in front of my eyes, the year that I had spent with this lovely woman.

Each moment . . . magic . . .

Every second . . . memorable . . .

∽

My first memory of her was perhaps from the time I was three—a beauty mole over her lips, thick, short hair, a round bindi on her forehead and a smile. NALINI DUTTA.

My Ma . . .

My parents, Nalini and Surinder Dutta, were both doctors. Both were also ardent fans of Dilip Kumar. They had been college sweethearts. I was told that when Ma had first gone to meet Dad's sisters in Delhi, they had said, 'She's lovely but a bit overweight!'

For her dear Surinder, Nalini lost about 15 kg before marriage and the sisters-in-law were pleased, of course, to have a pretty, thin bhabhi!

Fortunately, both of them got posted in the rural areas of Punjab after marriage. They took on their assignments with full enthusiasm.

Though Ma and Dad were known to be the ideal couple, their personalities were poles apart. Dad was a quiet, sober, idealistic man and Ma, well, er . . . not so quiet. She was full of life, super confident and practical. If Dad found it difficult to communicate with someone, which was most of the time as he was very shy, Ma, without mincing words, would do the needful. Sometimes, just sometimes, putting Dad in an awkward situation by communicating more than was necessary! She did it without realizing it though.

Dad, being at a more senior position at the hospital, would often ask for a written explanation from Ma if she was late for duty by even five minutes. Ma wondered why she couldn't get some leniency sometimes, especially when I came along. But Dad would have none of it and they would argue like little kids. But they loved each other very much. If anyone else said anything to Ma, Dad was always by her side, protectively defending her.

I am told that when I was born in Amritsar in my buanani's (grandaunt's) hospital it was as if Ma and Dad had got married again. There was a huge, wedding-like celebration. I was the firstborn in both sides of the family. Ma had been praying a lot for a baby girl at the Darbar Saheb. She used to do a lot of *sewa* there—she would sweep the floor, make rotis, wash utensils. She had taken a *mannat*, to be blessed with a girl, at the Dukhbhanjan Beri. She had decided on my name beforehand—Divya, at that time a very exclusive name. Such was Ma.

I was the apple of their eyes, of course, but also the reason for their arguments. They were a set of over-cautious parents who would get worried even if I cried for a bit. I just had to make a sound for Dad to get worried and scold Ma for not checking on me. Ma would tense up too, if I cried. Poor Ma. I would just cling on to her, literally.

If she left me even for a second, I would start shrieking. And then both of them would start off all over again. One would wonder who, out of the three, was the baby. But I remember my growing up years with great fondness. Those days were simple and much of what we did circled around the hospital Ma and Dad worked in. We played in the hospital compound, we ate together, then we went for scooter rides. My parents made sure that their bachcha was a happy child, and I was. When

I look back, I think life was beautiful then—just like it is in the movies.

I still remember the Manoj Kumar–Nanda song with the little boy.

'*Ek pyar ka nagma hai; maujon ki rawani hai* . . . (It's a song of love; it's the ebb and flow of tides . . .)'

Zindagi aur . . . kuch bhi nahi, teri–meri kahani hai . . . (Life is nothing but your and my story . . .)'

Yes. Zindagi then was all about being with Ma and Dad and living our sweet kahani.

2

Stepping into the World

§

I was really nervous on my first day of school. The Sacred Heart Convent was the biggest and the best school in Ludhiana in those days. Dad and Ma had come to drop me on Dad's Lambretta scooter. How I loved standing in front of Dad on that scooter! The breeze brushing past my face and my parents behind me, I felt like a princess who owned the world. Blissful.

When I got off the scooter, the school building loomed large in front of me and I felt like I was stepping into another world. So many children, so much noise and hustle-bustle that I immediately felt lost. I looked back at my parents and Ma said, 'We will be right here waiting for you.' She smiled.

I felt reassured. With a heavy heart, I went into the class. All the kids were laughing, chatting and playing. It looked like fun. But I was too eager to go back to my parents who were waiting for me, go to my favourite ice cream shop with them and then go home and play with Sindro, our domestic help's daughter, who I'd become very close to. Somehow I settled in, feeling alone amongst the many children.

Finally, when the school bell rang I ran out, looking for Ma and Dad. Dad had decided to play a prank on me and he asked Ma to hide. I kept looking around. *Where were they? How could they have not waited for me? Why had they left without me when Ma had promised?* My little mind was filled with scary thoughts and my anguish knew no bounds. Then suddenly I felt a warm embrace. It was Ma! She had sensed my panic and immediately came and hugged me.

I pushed her away, howling, 'Never, ever leave me alone like that, never . . .'

She hugged me tighter and said, 'Never, beta, never ever . . .'

She never did. In fact her support is what I could always count on, no matter what.

Ma called me her princess and I believed I was one. So one day, when the school teacher came to class to cast for the role of a princess for the annual day play, the little me sat there confidently, thinking I was the right person for it. As the teacher took rounds of the class to pick 'the prettiest of them all', I knew she'd come and stop in front of me. But she stopped even before reaching my bench. The girl in front of me was asked to get up. And she was chosen!

I was heartbroken.

The teacher had missed selecting the real princess. She hadn't even looked at me. Maybe she hadn't seen me. So I made one last effort. I raised my hand and said, 'Ma'am, I'm here!'

She looked at me, very amused, and said, 'No, child. I've found my princess.'

Needless to say, I was howling. I also went back to Ma to report about the teacher who didn't seem to know my 'real' identity. I was inconsolable.

Ma sat me on her lap and wiped the tears off my face. 'Divu beta,' she said gently, 'you are my princess. Exclusively, only for me. Why would I share such a lovely princess with the teacher? You rule my world and you are needed here. So brighten my world. And let the teacher cast you in another role another time.'

Those words made the five-year-old me understand the mystery behind it all. Yes, I was the real princess. Ma's princess, so special and so loved. Yeah, I could probably let the teacher choose me for something else, another time.

Until then, I was happy sitting on this lap, my kingdom.

3

A Sweet Baby Boy for Me!

We were all at the Golden Temple—Ma's sisters, Saloni and Aruna, the latter's little daughter, Jyotica, Ma with a fat belly and I. I was told that a baby would come out of her belly and he/she was coming especially for me, to be my best friend. I would keep looking at the protruding stomach, wondering why the baby was taking so long to get out.

Anyway, we were all having langar, the community food served in gurudwaras. I loved the way Ma made me fold my hands in gratitude when the roti was served. It felt beautiful. I was busy polishing off the food when I heard an urgent discussion among the three sisters. The masis looked worried. One masi held my Ma's hand and hurried towards the exit. The other masi held me and Jyotica, and we followed them. The sudden hurry puzzled me. Ma looked restless and I ran to be with her. Her hand was on her stomach.

We were back at my grandaunt's hospital. We were waiting in the lobby when Dad told me my baby was arriving! All mine . . . my new best friend.

Minutes later, in true filmy style, the nurse came out with a little bundle in her arms. Dad gestured her to put it on my lap. As he lay crying in my lap, I noticed the cutest face, just like Dad's, and small hands like my doll's. Dad sat next to me and whispered in my ears, 'That's your baby brother! Now take care of him like a big sister.'

I felt so protective looking into those beautiful, angelic eyes. Yeah, I knew he was going to be my best friend.

My cousin, Jyotica, who is my age, came running to pick him up too, and I remember I didn't let her. 'You'll drop him! He's so tiny and you are too small to handle him!' I said possessively.

She gave me an angry look. I knew she could have punched my nose but I couldn't care less. This angel was mine.

We named him Rahul—again a very exclusive name back then (now, of course, the most overused one!).

I would see Ma take care of little Rahul. That is when I started experiencing slight pangs of jealousy. She fed him, massaged him, changed his clothes, sang lullabies to him. I would look at the two of them and feel left out.

To get Ma's attention, I would go sit on her lap when she was busy with Rahul and demand, 'You sing me my favourite song too!'

Ma would look helpless. Dad noticed all the conflicted feelings his Gugu was experiencing. I had started doing things to grab attention. I would not eat food, throw Rahul's toys and run away.

One day when I came back from school, I saw both Ma and Dad sitting with Rahul, waiting for me. Dad told me he and Ma had to go out for some urgent work and that I'd have to look after Rahul. I protested immediately. I wasn't going to look after him! He had taken away Ma from me!

Dad reminded me of what I had promised him earlier. That I'd be the big sister. That I'd take care of him.

I relented unwillingly.

I sat with baby Rahul as Ma and Dad left the room.

I left some toys with him and sat in a corner reading my comics. I heard him cry but I chose to ignore him. He was crawling towards me. I looked away. I had decided I wouldn't bother about him at all.

Suddenly, I felt his little hands tug at me, his cute toothless smile inviting me to play with him. Something happened within me. I felt like playing with him too, but then I had promised myself not to give in.

Those little hands snatched my comics and he looked at me again. His arms spread, gesturing me to lift him up. It was his initiative at friendship. And this time I couldn't stop myself and the gesture was duly reciprocated. I lifted him up and cuddled him tight. Sheer joy! Yes that's what I felt.

Once on my lap, he began to smile. So did I. I brought all his toys and started playing with him. We were both laughing and having fun. Later, I changed his nappy and gave him his milk bottle, just like Ma would. I was the elder protective sister after all! I realized he was adorable. He wasn't my rival! He wasn't to be envied. Ma and I both could give him love. Together. He was the younger one and he needed it more than I did. Anyway, Ma and Dad loved me so much and trusted me that they'd given me the responsibility of looking after him. It was my turn to live up to that trust.

I took him in my arms and sang my favourite song to him. I folded his hands in the same way Ma had taught me in the gurudwara.

In gratitude.

Unknown to me at that time, somewhere behind the door, Ma and Dad were looking at the scene and smiling . . .

4

Two Journeys and One Goodbye

§

Bags had been packed. Dad was going to London to join a hospital in the ophthalmology department. If everything went the way he had planned, Ma, my six-month-old brother, Rahul, and I too, could join him in a while. I sat with Rahul on my lap, cheerfully saying bye to Dad, thinking he would come back soon with lots of toys for us. I was too young to feel his absence immediately. However, after he left, it did start sinking in how much I was going to miss him.

Dad used to send occasional parcels for us. But what I really looked forward to were not the toys but the postcards that would arrive from him. He wrote beautiful notes for his Gugu, telling me how much he missed me and talking about all the places he would show me when I visited him. I would keep the postcards in my closet, not even sharing them with Ma. But soon even those postcards weren't enough. They couldn't fill the void that his departure had created. I started missing him more. His bedtime stories, scooter rides with him, me sitting on his shoulders and playing, his teaching me how to sing . . . I craved for everything.

Then one day, when I was visiting my favourite cousin's house with Ma and Rahul, I saw her playing with her father. I kept looking at the two of them for a while and then the six-year-old me went up to my uncle and blurted out, 'Till my daddy comes back, can I call you Daddy?'

There was pin-drop silence. No one said anything. My cousin stopped playing with her father.

Such an episode could not have been lightly taken by Ma. This incident was immediately reported to Dad. I don't know what conversation ensued between them on the phone, but Dad was back the very next month. He had quit the job in London and came back to join the hospital in Sahnewal again. He had decided to be with his baby girl. I was over the moon with excitement. The void that I had felt for so long suddenly disappeared. He was back to fill it with all his love. Life finally came back on track for all of us.

～

Mom and Dad were very busy doctors and there used to be long queues of patients waiting outside their hospital wards. I felt so proud to be the child of such in-demand doctors. Quite naturally, I was given a lot of importance and was pampered by the patients too. Of course, I loved it. To add to my important status, I was also the in-house pundit. Many believed that my prediction of whether the expecting parents would have a baby girl or a baby boy would be spot on. Well I had no idea from where I got such a sixth sense but I did not have to give much thought to my predictions. They seemed to work and I would bask in all the attention. That is all that mattered! After school, I would spend all my time at the hospital. Honestly, life couldn't have been better!

However, spending all my spare time with the patients had its repercussions and one soon came to the forefront. One evening, as Dad sat with me and went through my homework, he realized I hadn't done anything. He was taken aback. He asked me the reason and was shocked to hear my new style of speaking. I had picked up some colourful cuss words from the staff and the patients, and I was now trying them on Dad. To my utter surprise he wasn't pleased at all! His Gugu was learning bad words and he had been too busy to even notice that. He looked sad and forlorn. I, on the other hand, still couldn't understand what had gone so drastically wrong.

Later that night, I heard Ma and Dad have an argument. I was in my room but I could hear my name being taken several times. I got scared. I kept wondering, what had I done so wrong that Ma and Dad were unhappy and fighting over me? Suddenly, the door opened and Ma came in with swollen eyes. It seemed she had been crying. Soon enough, Dad came and picked me up, 'Beta, can Daddy talk to you?'

The tone in his voice did not calm my fears. I just looked at him with bated breath. He continued softly, 'I came back especially for you, but I feel we should send you to your buas' [my father's sisters'] house in Delhi for some time. We want to send you away from this atmosphere so you can get groomed better. This place is not for you, my child. I will bring you back soon, I promise . . .'

Ma was looking at Dad, disagreement writ large in her eyes. But Dad had decided.

I could never forgive him for taking me away from him, Ma and baby Rahul. From my home. I didn't want to go anywhere. Even though I promised him repeatedly that I wouldn't ever use those cuss words, Dad did not budge. For the first time, my father didn't listen to me. He remained adamant. 'We will come and meet you as often as possible. My Gugu is going away to become a very good girl.'

Those words didn't provide much solace.

That fateful night, I sat on Ma's lap for a very long time, hoping some miracle would take place and Dad would change his mind.

Nothing of the sort happened.

Soon after, my school admissions in Delhi were done and my bags were packed. It was time to say goodbye. All I could muster as I left my house was 'Ma' as I pulled at her dupatta and took it with me. It had her fragrance ... her presence ...

I didn't talk to Dad throughout the journey and ate only Ma's paranthas. No amount of offers of ice creams or cold drinks by Dad could entice me. It was a mark of rebellion. I would always be *katti* with Dad for taking me away from my little world, from Ma. One thing the little me had decided, I would never speak to him.

5

My Stay in Delhi

§

Dad and I reached his sisters' house in Delhi. He stayed with me for a few days and then left. I was still sulking. It was difficult for me to stay without my immediate family, especially Ma. But, however slowly, life always moves on. My buas made every effort to make me feel at home. There was an overdose of pampering. After all, there were three of them, all single, as none of them had married. Two of them were teachers in government schools. So they took it upon themselves to teach me too. My third bua was a lot into fashion and films. She would give me new hairstyles every day. Sometimes a Neetu Singh fringe, other times a Hema Malini ponytail or Zeenat Aman plaits. She knew I was a film buff and she would convince me into believing that after those hairdos, I did look like those heroines. She was partially successful in lifting my spirits. I, all of seven at that time, though occasionally happy with such indulgences, hadn't adjusted to my new surroundings yet. I was a rebel with a cause. I wanted to go back to my house, my family . . . my Ma.

One afternoon, after I got back from school, there was a knock at the door. It was the peak of the Delhi summer. Who would have come at that hot hour of the day? Didn't people have any work? I kept mumbling as I went and opened the door. I couldn't believe my eyes! I was absolutely shocked. It was Ma! She was standing there with her arms open wide to hug me. All she said was, 'I had to see you, *bas, train pakdi aur aagayi* (I just caught the train and came)!'

I literally jumped at her, making it very difficult for her to even go inside. Tightly hugging each other, with me on her lap, we both sat on the couch for a few minutes without uttering a single word. That silence had its own magic. It happens when the hearts are full. As ours were. I didn't want the moment to end. The silence was finally broken by my buas who looked equally surprised at seeing Ma in their house without any prior notice. Even they hadn't known Ma was coming.

On enquiring about her sudden visit, Ma said she would leave the very next day as she hadn't taken leave from the hospital. When I heard she was leaving so soon, the rush of happiness that I had felt somewhat dissipated. It was too short a time to spend with Ma. I just couldn't get enough of looking at her. I wanted to be with her. I only wished she had come to take me back with her.

As my mind was trapped in a tumult of emotions, Ma opened her little bag and out came some beautiful *ghagra–choli*s, and Western dresses. 'I have been shopping for my little angel, I want you to look the best and feel the best!'

I took the gifts, not knowing what to say. Of course, I was happy on seeing her and all those gifts but I would have felt better if I could have returned home with her. But that didn't happen. Ma reasoned patiently with me. I was in the midst of the academic session and there was no way I could leave midway.

I had no choice.

Ma had this knack of giving me surprises. Like a genie she'd appear when I really wished she was around.

In one such instance, many years later, at a summer camp in Manali, I was with my college mates doing the morning PT. It had been quite a few days since I had met Ma and I had been pretty homesick. I was desperately waiting for the camp to wrap up. I couldn't believe what I saw. At the far end of the hill, I saw a familiar face. *No, it couldn't be!* I thought I was hallucinating and that my mind was playing mean tricks with me. *It couldn't be Ma!* After a few minutes, I saw another familiar face. It was Rahul's and then another, my nani's.

They were all there and they were all smiling as I stood frozen in sheer disbelief.

Do dreams really come true like this? At least Ma always managed to make them come true for me. There I was, just staring at them, too stunned to say anything. She walked up to the teacher first and announced, 'We thought we will personally come and give our daughter the good news that she's been selected to represent India in Japan. She's cleared the interview at the Red Cross Society.'

That day, for the first time in my life, I realized what tears of happiness meant.

Ma came up to me and hugged me. After a while, they all left. It felt like a dream. Even now, sometimes I hear a knock at the door. Maybe I hallucinate in the hope of catching a glimpse of her smiling face and her saying, 'I just thought I will see you . . .'

Still waiting for this surprise, Ma . . .

6

Tragedy Strikes

§

I had spent three years in Delhi. During the course of this time, I had made some good friends, played with them, cracked jokes together, and laughed away all my worries. I had finally settled in and was indeed very happy there. To add to my happiness, my father was visiting the next day. He had promised to attend my annual function at school. After so many days I would be seeing him. There were no words to express my excitement. It would be so much fun to attend the function with Dad, I thought. I was yearning for him to call me Gugu. I absolutely loved the way he said it.

However, destiny has its own way of tricking people.

As I was making my grand plans with my father, I heard my bua's voice from the other end of the house, 'Divuuu . . . trunk call from Punjab . . . come fast . . .' She was calling me.

It must be Ma who is calling to tell me what time Dad would reach, I thought with great excitement. I ran fast. I had to talk to Ma and Dad before that trunk call got disconnected. I also wanted to give them a list of the things I wanted Dad to bring and, of course, send a big kissie to little Rahul. I was going through this list in my head when I reached the phone. I saw my bua was staring at me with the receiver still in her hand. She said nothing. I literally snatched it from her. The call had been disconnected. I had missed talking to Ma and Dad. I looked at bua again, shocked by her behaviour. But before I could question her, she hugged me tight. She was crying. What was the big deal about a phone getting disconnected? I wondered. They would call again, I was sure of that. Why was she so upset? Why had all my buas suddenly started crying?

My eldest aunt mumbled, 'We are leaving for Sahnewal right now.'

Oh! So, the plan had changed! I would now go and meet all three of them . . . Dad, Ma and Rahul.

Bua immediately interrupted my thoughts, 'Your dad's left us . . . he's no more . . .!' she wailed.

I stood numb.

No, I did not register a word she said.

What was she saying? Was she in her senses? How could Dad leave without meeting me? He had promised to come. I stood there dumbfounded. I was still in shock even when my things were packed and I was made to sit in the car.

During the seven-hour journey, I kept thinking about him not showing up. We were to attend the annual day hand in hand. He was to take me back home with him and he'd just left. How could he?

At midnight, we reached Sahnewal. I saw Ma at the entrance waiting for us. She looked devastated, nothing like the lovely Ma I knew. She saw me and hugged me tight. My little hands wiped her tears, which refused to stop. She took us inside.

There he was, lying still. Right in the centre of the living room. I went and sat next to him, thoughts ruling my mind. He would always hug me tight when he saw me. In that very room, we'd played blind man's bluff. And when it would be my turn, he would pick me and lift me up in the air. And I would laugh. 'Mera Gugu . . .' he would call out.

He must be feeling cold on that ice slab. It was all I could think of. Ma sat quietly in the corner after receiving us. She wasn't looking anywhere. Stone-eyed, with the two-year-old Rahul on her lap, she sat all night in that corner and I sat looking at her.

It was the end of the days when I laughed with both Dad and Ma. My hope of coming back home to my family, to Rahul, Ma and Dad was also over. Just like a dream.

Life would never be the same again.

The week went by with people pouring in. Dad was the favourite doctor in town. Quietly, with earnestness, they repeated, '*Shareef insaan the* . . . (He was a sincere man . . .)'

Ma was feeding Rahul when a few neighbourhood women came by, 'Behenji, remove your bangles and wear white clothes now,' they said matter-of-factly.

That was the first time I saw Ma break down. I was so scared.

Was I going to lose her too?

A lady came and consoled her. Another gave her a glass of water. I tried reaching out to her in that crowd of women surrounding her but I was pushed out, away from her. In a few minutes, I heard my Ma's determined voice, 'I am not going to wear white clothes—my husband wouldn't have liked it. I am not going to mourn anymore. I have to look after my kids, and I will start work tomorrow, thanks for coming,' she said with such authority that it shut those ladies up.

That day Ma took on the role and responsibility of Dad too.

The very next day she was at her hospital ward, seeing patients, looking after Rahul and me, taking charge of the entire situation. That is exactly what Dad would have liked her to do. That was her tribute to her husband, her college sweetheart, whom she loved madly.

Twenty days had passed and it was time for me to go back to Delhi. I sat in my room quietly when Ma came and sat next to me. She requested my buas, 'Can I please keep Divya here?'

My buas looked at me. Given the situation, they couldn't say anything. I just hugged Ma tightly and then went up to my buas, saying, 'I need to be with her now. I will stay back.' I could feel at that moment I had spoken like Ma. With an authority in my voice that no one could say no to.

I took Ma's hand in my little hands, 'Ma, I will be with you, always . . .'

She looked at me, overwhelmed.

Somewhere I could feel Dad smiling.

Somewhere I heard my name, *Gugu*.

Somewhere I knew I was doing something right.

7

A Feisty Mother and a
Devoted Child

§

Ma, Rahul and I returned to Delhi to do my final packing. Ma was trying to normalize life for us and would occasionally take us out.

I still remember the time she took us to the picnic spot around India Gate. For us, although it was exciting to have ice creams and go on fun rides, the biggest attraction was boating next to India Gate. *Bas, bachchon ki farmaish*—the kids' demand— Ma didn't have a choice. It had to be fulfilled anyhow! Ma held both us kids and led us to the booking booth for the boat ride. It was extremely crowded. Finally, after what seemed like an eternity, our turn came. We finally got the tickets and headed towards the boats. The boat was full already. The boatman, as if only going about his job, lifted my kid brother and dumped him on another kid's lap. When it was my turn to set foot on the boat, he suddenly decided to have no more people aboard. 'The boat is full, no more kids, your daughter can take the next one.'

Ma was furious. She insisted that both her children were to enjoy the ride together. Not interested in listening to her, he started moving the boat. Rahul looked on helplessly as he was being taken away without his sister. I, the sister, looked helplessly at not being able to join him. The people around showed a bit of concern but nobody bothered to do anything about it! Only one person could, and she did!

Before the boat could move too far away, my Ma put her foot on the boat, stopping it from moving ahead! So her one foot was on the dock and the other was stopping the boat. Just like Superman! Everyone was staring at what was happening. 'Not without my daughter!' she yelled.

The boatman was an egoistic man. He didn't bother about the poor lady swinging between land and water, fighting for her children's rights and moved the boat with full force as if competing with Ma. The inevitable happened. My dear Ma lost her balance and fell into the water! That was it—I could no longer watch from the sideline. I had to save my mother from drowning even though I was just a ten-year-old and didn't even know the S of swimming. Anyway, one cannot question emotions. So I jumped into the water yelling, 'Ma, Ma! Save her!'

There was frenzy all around. Two people were now drowning because of a boatman who still looked undeterred. I was trying to save Ma by holding her tight and she was splashing around in the water continuously. Rahul looked like he had lost everything in that one moment. He was helplessly bidding us goodbye.

The boatman had had enough of this drama. He alighted from the boat and got into the water. As he stood straight, everyone realized that the water level was only three-feet deep. So, after all the furore we realized that we were not drowning! It was mere panic.

Soon we were, not so politely, guided back to the dock by the boatman. I was extremely embarrassed but Ma wasn't. She never was! She was still waging her war with the boatman, 'Give me my child back! I don't want him on your boat!'

The stubborn man finally relented. He brought the boat back to the dock and out came Rahul. He ran to us to unite with his long-parted family.

As we moved away from the staring eyes, my little embarrassed self could only hear Ma's voice, 'Don't worry! Let me take you to another boat where both of you can sit together!'

I looked up at her and marvelled at the lady who could do anything to bring a smile on her kids' faces.

I was not embarrassed anymore. She held my hand tight. That grip told me I was safe, *sab theek hai jab hum saath saath hain* (everything is okay because we are together).

And we were . . .

8

The Day I Grew Up . . .

So I came back home to Ma and Rahul. And to nani who had also come to live with us. I shifted back to the school I used to go to earlier, the Sacred Heart Convent. Same classmates, same teachers— everything became the same, but without realizing it, I had changed a bit. I had subconsciously become very dependent on my buas for every little thing—getting ready, studying, packing my school bags. I didn't know how to do anything myself anymore. I used to bring all the homework to Ma and sit there looking at her. 'Teach me!' I would insist. She obliged for a few days, but then she sat me down with some strict advice, 'You are in the sixth standard. You are now a grown-up, my girl! Do your work yourself at least! And then help me with the house! It will be nice for my daughter to be my strength.'

This really shook me and hit me hard. I grew up that day. I realized how much Ma needed me. For what other reason had I come back if I couldn't be there for her? From then on, I started doing my own little things by myself, helping Ma and nani whenever they needed me, and most importantly, being with Ma when I felt she was alone! I managed studying all the subjects myself and getting good marks but maths failed me, literally!

I'll never forget the day of the eighth standard result. It was the first and last time Ma ever slapped me. Despite scoring well in the rest of the subjects, I had failed miserably in maths. She didn't speak to me for a few days. Maybe she was angry with me or with herself for slapping her baby.

I was very upset. Not for being slapped but because I had upset Ma. I had disappointed her. What was it that I couldn't get about maths? What was the big deal about those boring numbers? I went up to Ma, 'Sorry, yaar, last time please! I won't ever let you down Ma, promise!' That was all I could get myself to say. Tears soon welled up in my eyes and I started crying. The very next moment, I found myself in her lap, in her arms. Maybe we were both waiting for the other to say something and finish the incident with a hug.

From then on, there was no looking back. I become an all-rounder and an independent girl. From being the house captain to the best actor and dancer in school, I was a topper at everything! I ended up topping my class in languages and getting 78 per cent in maths. I had scored well in the subject! From then on, I bid goodbye to my dear mathematics because I was soon going to move to college and would have a free hand to choose my favourite subjects.

Ma also believed in me getting a holistic training and perfecting every sphere in life. She had put me under the able guidance of her chef to learn cooking, the best tailor in Sahnewal taught me stitching and her driver gave me driving practice.

Being a female driver was extremely rare those days. At this point I'd like to add a little about Ma's driving skills. She belonged to another category of drivers. She was, to put it mildly, a hilariously terrible driver. But despite that, we used to be proud to sit with her when she drove. The entire market area and neighbourhood, in consideration of their own safety, would keep a half-mile distance when she drove past. Ma did not know the concept of brakes. All she was aware of was the accelerator in her Fiat car. The tyres made screeching noises, helplessly finding their way out of potholes. Ma, without a care in the world, greeted people as she drove by. The brake was used only once, to stop at the hospital for her duty!

But she made sure her daughter would have better road skills. Once we were to catch an early morning train to Delhi during winter but as we reached the station, we realized that the train had already left. We were late by a mere five minutes. Our faces fell. If we had to book our tickets all over again, our vacation would get wasted. We sat there in silence, mourning for the spoilt vacation.

'Why don't you drive us to Delhi?' Ma asked me calmly.

I looked at her in disbelief. 'Who, me? Absolutely not!'

She said again, 'Why? You have a valid licence, and I am sitting with you. What are you scared of? We'll keep stopping every now and then to enjoy the journey.'

I looked at Rahul for some support but he nodded and agreed with Ma. What kind of a supportive family was this! I had started driving well but I had never driven on the highway. That too, on a two-way Grand Trunk Road with huge trucks plying round-the-clock. But with the confidence they showed in me, I didn't want to let them down. In fact I wanted to prove them right and make it one hell of a fun journey!

However, it was easier said than done. The moment I landed up with the car on the super busy GT Road, I froze.

'*O chal na* (C'mon drive)!' my Punjabi mother said. '*Bas, meri tarah mat chalana* (Just don't drive like me)!'

We all laughed and I somehow relaxed. She had effortlessly eased out my nervousness. Before I knew it, I was driving like a pro, finding and manoeuvring my way through the trucks, buses and speeding cars. We stopped at the Karnal picnic spot, had our lunch, Ma's favourite *aloo ki sabzi* and paranthas, did some boating and started again. Not once during the whole journey did I feel that I was driving for the first time on this dangerous road. Ma didn't let me.

Before we resumed our journey, I stole a glimpse of Ma. She was happily having her paranthas and chatting with Rahul. How easy someone could make every journey of your life by their mere presence, by their words! How important this reassurance is in one's life, to know that this someone is right behind you even if you fall. Empowered with this reassurance, even the fall feels like a fun adventure.

Thanks you so much, Ma, my life's best coach!

9

The Curfew Days

§

There was pin-drop silence in the usually busy market outside our house. No shops were open, there were no vehicles or people around. The quiet was eerie. I peeped out of my balcony. There was no one except a few patrolling army men. It was curfew time in Punjab. For us kids, it was initially an exciting time since school was shut but after a few days it got boring and scary. The lack of normality soon got to us. What could one possibly do just sitting in the house for so many days. Our neighbourhood uncle had bought a new VCR and he would invite all the kids to watch films. Or we would just play at home.

We ran between terraces to smuggle in grocery from our neighbourhood grocer while Ma would send the neighbours medicines through us. In this way, the community would help each other out. Since Ma was the local civil surgeon she had to be on duty 24 x 7 in case of an emergency. I used to feel so scared when she left for work, her jeep disappearing on the empty roads. While she was away, I would keep staring into the empty space, dreading that I might hear some gunshots somewhere.

It had already happened once. Ma had to urgently reach the hospital but her jeep had broken down on the way. She left the driver and a class-four employee behind to repair it as everything was shut and she stood on the deserted road to ask for a lift. No one came for a while until an Ambassador appeared. It stopped where Ma was standing. It had four men inside. Ma was surprised to see a car on the road, given the curfew, but she had to reach the hospital so she requested them to drop her till the next village. There was a silent pause and then they nodded. They made Ma sit in the front seat. There was absolute silence in the car until Ma broke it by asking them where they were headed. No reply came from them. Ma became quiet, too, after that and soon the car came to a stop. They asked Ma to get off at the outskirts of the village as they wouldn't go in. Ma thanked them and left . . .

She had barely reached the village when she heard gunshots. The bodies of those same four men were brought to her hospital. They were terrorists shot in a chase just a few minutes after they had dropped Ma. Just a few minutes back, Ma was with them . . .

Hearing her recount that episode gave me goose bumps. It was the most relieving feeling to have her safe and back with us, hearing her voice instructing her staff as usual as she entered the gate to our house.

She never looked scared to me. She would always say, '*Oh kuch nai, kuch nai, mai hun na* (Don't you worry, I am there)!'

One evening, a letter was delivered to our house that created pandemonium. It was a threat letter which said that the doctor's children would be kidnapped unless a ransom was paid. Ma looked like she was going to take on the perpetrators with her bare hands! She called up the police, who turned up on our doorstep immediately. The policeman who called was a tall, well-built guy who looked very dependable. He came in and patted Rahul on the back and told both of us not to worry. The beautiful thing was that people from the entire neighbourhood came home, ready to do anything for their doctor saheba and her kids! After all, Ma had been there in their hours of need always. She had saved their precious ones with her prescriptions!

In a very filmy scenario, the police, Ma and a few neighbours hid at the spot mentioned in the letter for the exchange of the ransom. We were left at home, tucked in safely with nani and Ma's staff.

We waited at home with bated breath, crossing our fingers that Ma would be safe. Hours passed by . . . and then I finally heard my mother's voice! It was such a relief! She was surrounded by the cops, neighbours and two handcuffed boys! Yes, the criminals were caught . . .

I just looked at Ma. She was my iron lady, a woman of sheer grit. I am sure she had fears, of being the only woman with the police and neighbours while waiting for the miscreants; of losing her kids; of something happening to her; for the future of her children . . . but she showed none of it! She only displayed her undiluted strength to fight the situation . . . to face the problem head on and solve it. And she did! With natural ease.

After everyone left, she asked for her regular black elaichi chai in a steel tumbler. That was her way of relaxing. And she sat holding us . . . she knew what had passed was tough on us and we were still nervous. Her soothing touch did wonders for us.

A surprise awaited us the next day. Ma had packed our bags and Rahul and I were to leave Punjab for a few days till everything got back to normal. Her work required her to stay back.

I hated leaving her and nani alone. But when she decided on something, we knew we had to abide by it.

We were going to visit our masi. Ma packed a lots of goodies for my masi's kids . . . and for us.

We sat in the jeep waving to her. She soon disappeared in the dust that rose from the speeding tyres . . . or may be it was tears . . .

10

College Days and a New Beginning

§

My personal view is that when you are given the opportunity of choosing the subjects that you like, your studies become enjoyable. This is exactly what happened to me and that was the reason I topped in college in all my subjects— philosophy, psychology and English. This was also possible because of Ma. She never pressurized me to become a doctor like her, or to follow in her footsteps. She let me walk my own path.

Given my exceptional achievements in academics, I had been granted a scholarship in college. I was happy and proud. However, in spite of this, exams remained the most gruelling time for me. I have to confess here that I had a very bad habit of lying down on my bed and studying. As a result, one moment I was studying and the next, I would have dozed off!

This clearly was not helping my preparations. Once when my exams were not too far, I began my studies in earnest but I kept dozing off every day. The result was that I lagged behind. There was a lot of studying left to be done and I was losing time. Ma had had enough of this lethargic attitude. She came into my room one day and said strictly, 'Sit and study. Don't lie down!'

I teasingly told her, 'So find me a place where I have no option of lying down!'

'Go to the bathroom,' she retorted.

This actually made a lot of sense to me. On the terrace we had a huge, unused bathroom. So, I decided on that exclusive venue! The bathroom was cleaned up especially for me. The bucket was the table and instead of towels, the racks were used to keep my books. Everyone knew where I could be found when I was in total study mode. I used to shut myself there for hours, trying to compensate for the lost time. Not lying down and studying made it easier for me to grasp more and be alert. I started enjoying studying in there. After all, I was also studying all my favourite subjects. I felt so motivated. The goal became clearer to me. The aim was to continue getting my scholarship.

The only time I left the bathroom was for lunch so Ma always made sure that her hardworking daughter got only her favourite items for lunch.

The film buff that I was, I had a weird habit of reading a film magazine while eating. One day, I laid my hands on the latest issue of *Stardust* magazine. Casually flipping through the pages, I came across an entry form for a talent hunt by *Stardust*. Of course, I loved acting. I daydreamed of being in front of the camera, of shooting with Amitabh Bachchan, of dancing around trees, of walking up the stage to receive my best actor award . . .

How could this dream ever be fulfilled for a small-town girl? This talent hunt was a ray of hope and I didn't want to miss the opportunity. So, the very same day I took a break from my studies and asked my eleven-year-old brother to click a few pictures of me. I wore my most glamorous dresses, imagining myself as Miss World and posed like I was the next big thing to happen to Bollywood.

For me, the entire photoshoot was an amazing experience, so lovingly done by my dear brother who clicked me with full zest, making me sit at the most absurd places—on the parapet, on a sandbag, on a bicycle. Obviously, Rahul was thrilled to play this very important role I had bestowed upon him.

Gosh! Despite being sceptical of Rahul's abilities, I loved my pictures. In my opinion, they belonged to the cover page of *Stardust*. Rahul didn't seem very satisfied with his job though. But I posted the pictures along with the form to the designated address.

Given the attention span of a teenager, I soon forgot about it. I was back to my usual routine, studying hard for exams. Ma was very happy with my progress and the effort that I was putting in. Life was great. *Sab* smooth *tha* (everything was running smoothly).

After a few weeks, however, the most unexpected thing happened. We received a telegram from *Stardust*! They were calling me for an audition! My heart skipped a beat. Was it for real or was someone pulling a fast one on me?

Before I could take any decision of my own, I realized it was time to share this big news with Ma. Rahul and my little secret had to be disclosed. We were scared but it had to be done. So I finally gathered the courage and went to her. I handed her the telegram. Rahul stood beside me. She stared at me first, then in complete silence she carefully went through the telegram.

Those few seconds felt like an eternity to me.

'You seriously want to be an actor?' she asked.

I heard myself say, 'Yes, Ma.' The voice was coming from the core of my heart. 'I want to be an actor.' There was silence again. Rahul was staring at the floor, not daring to look up since he had played the role of an ace photographer. I kept looking at Ma.

She finally spoke, 'I'll never stop you from doing what you want to do, beta. As long as you are clear that it is what you want in life. But I want to warn you, it's not the easiest of professions. Also, everyone in our family wants you to study further as you are a very good student. But I'll not force others' expectations on you. If something gives you happiness, I'll be with you. But are you sure you want to take this path?'

Her words strengthened my belief even more. It suddenly hit me that there was nothing I wanted to do more than become an actor! That nothing gave me more happiness than performing and hearing the applause of the audience! My college performances were a testimony to that.

I spoke instantly, 'Yes, I want to pursue acting. Will you come with me for the audition?'

This time her reply came instantly. She had seen the twinkle in my eye.

'Okay, I'll come with you for the audition. But promise me that you'll not let your exams get affected by this. You'll study even harder and not leave that bathroom!'

She had agreed! She was going to support me, be by my side, hold my hand for something that wasn't going to be an easy journey.

We both soon realized that.

11

Auditions in Mumbai

§

Going to Mumbai for auditions wasn't the easiest thing to do. Now that Ma was on my side, I had to convince my nani. Her son, my uncle, Deepak Bahry, was a renowned film director of his time, having directed well-known films like *Taraana* and *Agent Vinod*. Ma gathered confidence from the fact that at least her brother was in Mumbai. Still, going for the audition was to be a secret. Unless, of course, I was selected. But what if I wasn't selected after all the *hungama*?

Nani was a stunningly beautiful blue-eyed woman. She was extremely fond of me but was a bit too practical and blunt for my good. So as soon as I broke the news to her that Ma and I were going to Mumbai for auditions, she was livid. She was sure I wouldn't get selected!

She pulled me aside and asked sternly, 'Have you both lost your minds? You got a crazy idea in your head and now your mother's supporting you! I am not with both of you in this decision. And you should be practical. You are not the typically tall and pretty type to be a heroine! Just study, be an IAS officer and get married!'

I was a bit shocked by her outburst but not shaken in my resolve.

In fact, as I walked away from her, I had a smile on my face. Something inside told me that Ma and I, the two crazy women, would make it.

So we both boarded the train to Mumbai and went to mama's house. He and his family, comprising his wife, two daughters and my nana, were very happy to see us, though a bit surprised. We'd not let out the real motive for the visit since my mama was a very conservative Punjabi man and for now there was no reason to alarm him.

I had prepared a mono-act, which Ma had written for the audition. I had performed it once at a college youth festival. So it was tried and tested.

I had bought a new salwar–kurti, which for me was very glamorous. Whatever little sense I had of make-up, I tried applying those skills on myself.

Finally, the audition day arrived. I had butterflies in my stomach. I was excited and nervous at the same time.

Like two buddies with a little secret, we left the house after giving a random excuse to the family. Ma was holding me tight to give me confidence, but I knew she was nervous too. It had taken a lot for her to stand up for me.

The taxi stopped at the venue of a five-star hotel.

Ma whispered in my ears, 'Hey, you remember your lines, na?'

I could sense the nervousness in her voice.

'Hmm . . .' I nodded.

We walked into the lobby and were directed towards a big hall. Outside the hall was a huge crowd of stunning-looking girls, tall and pretty. Some were so beautiful that I wondered if they were fairies who had dropped down from the skies.

Nani's words immediately came to my mind. 'You are not a typically beautiful girl to be a heroine!'

But I brushed those thoughts aside. I had to think positive. There was no other way. Ma and I, hand in hand, waited for my turn.

After an hour, that felt like an eternity, my name was announced. Ma's grip on my hand tightened.

She kissed my forehead and said, 'Give your dream your best!'

I was pleasantly surprised and nervous as I entered the hall.

In front of me sat a jury comprising the who's who of the industry—Shekhar Kapur, Subhash Ghai, Yash Chopra, Sooraj Barjatya . . . to name a few. For a minute I thought I would stop breathing. Directors whose films I had grown up watching, whose films were my world of fantasy, who I daydreamed of working with. They were all sitting together in the same room, waiting for me to perform. Imagine my condition! Seconds passed by and I was still staring at them in sheer disbelief. I even thought of running away from there.

But then those words of my mother resounded in my head: 'Give your dream your best!'

I don't know when I started performing. My legs were wobbly like jelly. My heart was pounding but there was something I was doing alongside. I was mouthing the lines written by Ma!

After the audition, they all smiled and Shekhar Kapur said they'd let me know in a few days. Like a zombie, I thanked them in a daze and came out.

Outside, even the editor of *Stardust* told Ma that he'd inform us about the results after a few days. Unsure and nervous, we came back home. We both knew it was going to be tough.

The next day we took a train to Ambala, where we were going to attend my cousin's wedding. Nani and Rahul would join us there.

We didn't speak much on the way to Ambala, both of us absorbing the moment we had been a part of.

Fortunately for us, the wedding ceremonies proved to be a distraction and we got engrossed in the singing and dancing. I got busy doing my favourite *thumka*s and Amitabh Bachchan steps and pulling everyone to join in too.

It was late evening when my uncle told nani that he wanted to have a word with me. I was certain that I would be pulled up for my enthusiasm in dancing with everyone. But it turned out to be a scene from a typical Hindi film.

My nani and uncle sat with my mother, waiting for me. Uncle held my hand and smiled and informed me that he had a *rishta* (an offer for marriage) for me. His friend's son had seen me dancing and had expressed his desire to marry me. He was a doctor settled in the US—a great catch for any Indian girl, especially in those days. He told me if I was ready, the boy would marry me immediately.

My nani was looking at me impatiently. She knew my little secret and about my dreams and where I had just returned from. She was sure it was an indulgence and nothing would come out of it. According to her, marriage to such a great match was the best decision. There were two people staring at me, waiting for me to say 'yes'. I chose to look at the third one sitting in the corner, silently asking her if she was with me.

Getting married at nineteen would put an end to my chances of becoming an actor. Even though my chances at succeeding were slim . . . what if . . . what if it did happen? I surely didn't want to live with a regret all my life . . .

I was trying to muster up the courage to say 'no'. A voice finally came out, but it wasn't mine— it was Ma's!

'*Nahin, bhai saab*, my daughter is too young to marry right now. I want her to give herself some time.'

Nani knew exactly what that meant. She walked out of the room, disappointed. Uncle also felt a bit let down.

Only two crazy women were left in the empty room and the older one spoke, 'Let's give your dream its best chance!'

Of course, that was indeed the answer I was looking for.

I don't remember having danced all night with so much happiness ever in my life. And yes, Ma was dancing with me too . . . matching each step.

12

How Destiny Changes Life in a Moment!

Days had passed by . . .

Ma and I had given up hope of the *Stardust* selection. In the meantime, life had been very kind to me. College days were turning out to be the best days of my life! I had become the head girl of my college. I had also been selected by the Red Cross Society to represent India in Japan. It was a great honour as only two girls from all over India had been selected for this talent exchange.

And what an absolutely enriching experience it had been! Debates, declamations, homestays, meeting new people.

I was welcomed back by the college with a lot of fanfare. My friends and teachers felt so proud of me. As did Ma.

Then it was time for the youth festivals again and I performed Ma's creation, the mono-act, and a folk dance. My days went in rehearsing and practising and also studying hard. Exams followed. Then came the time for the annual awards function to which parents were invited too. We were all in our black cloaks. I felt so proud to be in it. The best days were now going to be over! But there was a joy—an elation at having done something, of achievement.

As all good things do come to an end this was going to end too. But, some of it was still left . . .

The awards for the year were being announced. I had topped in all my subjects and received the best actor and dancer award too! I had to go up on the stage a couple of times to receive the trophies. Then came that beautiful moment when my principal, who was giving away the trophies, called my Ma up on the stage.

She announced, 'Why don't you announce this award, Dr Dutta?'

I was overwhelmed. So was Ma. We didn't know what the award was but she stood there with me on the stage and read the paper. My principal was smiling.

Ma read it out, 'And the award for the best all-round student of the year goes to . . .'

And she stopped short.

The tears had blurred out the words. But she knew the name.

My classmates gave a standing ovation. My teachers cheered along and my principal patted my back.

That trophy she gave to me and Ma!

I wish time had stopped then. I was the happiest to see Ma so happy.

Things did not end there. Soon everyone in college was worrying about the inter-university finale for the best actor competition to be held in Chandigarh.

At the Tagore Theatre in Chandigarh, all the four universities of Punjab participated in the competition, represented by their best actors. One of them was Gurpreet Ghuggi, a renowned Punjabi actor now, and another was Bhagwant Singh Mann, a comedian and an MLA now.

The mono-act Ma had scripted was to be tested once again, now in the grand finale.

I was the only female up against all the very popular boys.

I just looked at Ma and said, 'You wrote it so beautifully, Ma, I hope I can live up to it!'

Her expression after my performance said I had. There was a glint in her eyes, as if she was the one who had performed. She and I anyway were one entity, feeling the same emotions.

We exchanged nervous glances and waited for the result. I knew I had done well but there were more popular boys in the competition who had never lost.

Finally, the announcement came. Surprisingly, amidst unanimous cheer and applause from the students of all the universities, I, the underdog was declared the winner!

That coveted trophy was in my hands and I rushed down the stage to give it to my writer!

Ma was ecstatic too. I could see she was reminiscing about her college days, of being the most popular student and winning the best actor award in her youth festival. Those were her favourite days.

She was living it all over again through me. She was speechless but the glow on her face said it all.

When we reached home, we received a telegram. The news that had been long-awaited and now forgotten about had arrived too.

The nervous anticipation was back.

That was the thing about telegrams those days. You imagined a thousand horrible possibilities before those few seconds of opening and reading it. We both tried to read it together.

Hearts racing, we didn't know who was more nervous.

I stopped at the first word. 'Congratulations!' and then tried to reconfirm it by reading the rest—'You have been selected for the *Stardust* academy!'

I had finally made it!

From amongst 50,000 boys and girls all over India, that opportunity had knocked on my door!

A gamut of emotions surfaced. I was thrilled that my dream was going to be fulfilled. I had the chance to try my luck.

But my heart also clouded over with another emotion.

It was time to fly alone, to take the big plunge into the world of reality, leaving the protective surroundings of my home, my family, my Ma . . .

Ma read the telegram over and over again. She was going through the same emotions. Her young daughter had to now grow up and be on her own.

She sat me down. 'Divu, beta, congrats!' she said. 'So proud of you! Enjoy your training and your struggles! If you ever feel you want to come back, I'll be right here waiting for you.'

I hugged her tight and cried. The tears of joy of having such a supportive parent, of knowing she was always there, come what may, to hold me if I fell was overwhelming

I gave myself another award that day in my heart—of being the luckiest daughter in the whole world!

13

What a Heartbreaking Journey!

∾

The next big task now was to break the news to the family. Not that Ma wouldn't send me if anyone objected but she wanted to keep everyone informed. Nani already knew. She wasn't too happy with our decision as she thought I had a very bright future in academics but she gave her favourite grandchild her blessings nevertheless.

My buas, though, were livid! They thought we were committing a huge blunder. Once a girl entered the big bad world of films, she compromised her chances of finding a good match. Ma's faith in letting me take this opportunity was so strong that she eventually convinced them and soon everyone gave their nod.

However, some relatives did tell Ma that they'd sever all ties if she dared to send me to films. To them Ma smilingly said, 'No problem!'

The next biggest problem we had to deal with was breaking the news to my mama, Deepak Bahry. Ma wanted me to live in her brother's house and be taken care of by his family and feel the security of a home. Hence he needed to be taken into confidence. Also, since he was a producer–director himself, Ma was sure he would cast me in his movies. I bid Rahul and nani and the rest of the family a tearful goodbye. A new chapter was starting in my life. I had appeared for my final year exams as promised to Ma and the *Stardust* academy organizers had been kind enough to adjust the training dates with my exams as I was the editor's choice too.

Ma was obviously coming along to Mumbai to drop me. We boarded the train from the Ludhiana station. I was leaving behind my city, my home, to go to the city of dreams, to the vast unknown . . .

Being in Mumbai those first few days wasn't exactly a joy ride. As expected, no one in my mama's family was too thrilled about our decision. The '*ghar ki beti* (a girl in the family)' was planning to set foot in the film world . . . of course, they were apprehensive. But Ma remained undaunted. 'Okay, just look after my daughter till she completes her training so your sister feels her child has a home here,' she told them.

Mama, obviously, didn't say no to his dear sister and promised to take care of me.

Mama's dear friend, writer Suraj Sanim, who wrote most of Mahesh Bhatt's films and who later wrote a lot of Punjabi films that I worked in, used to regularly visit his home. He bonded with '*vadde bhenji* (older sister)' over poetry and Ma's favourite topic, her daughter. He also accompanied Ma to drop me at the academy at Madh Island.

Seven of us had been chosen from all over India to be trained and presented as *Stardust* protégés. It was a very big deal and Ma was nervous. Everyone at home wished us both good luck. It was a bigger decision for Ma than it was for me.

Finally, the three of us headed to the academy. No one spoke a word in the cab. After Dad's passing, I had hardly left Ma's side, the longest separation being when I had gone to Japan for a week. This was going to be a three-month training after which the so-called struggles would begin. It could last maybe a few months, or maybe forever. But I was going to be away from Ma for a long period, that was for sure.

I clasped her hand and kept it close to my chest, trying to feel and absorb her presence as much as I could, so it would at least stay on with me a few months. I promised myself to be brave and not break down in front of Ma. It had anyway been a tough, lonely ride for her. Ma also was doing the same. She knew that if she showed any signs of weakness, it would be difficult for me to leave.

We had reached the bungalow where the training was to be held. Sonali Bendre was one of the first students I saw there and I knew instantly we'd soon be very good friends.

Sonali helped me with my luggage but my attention stood firmly with the quiet figure whose life was going to change without me soon. She would have to say bye to her little best friend and to all the happy times spent together, the laughing, dancing, fighting and sharing . . . to good times and bad.

As a parent, the farewell was tougher for her but she didn't show it. She didn't come inside to drop me like she normally would have. She was fighting back her own tears. Surajji dropped me inside. I felt a little better knowing that Ma wasn't going back alone . . .

The cab sped away and I looked at it till it disappeared, leaving behind only a track of dust.

The dust of uncertainty that lay ahead . . .

14

Same Home, Different Life

§

I had completed my *Stardust* course but now the actual test had started or what was more appropriately called 'the struggle'. Coming from an extremely protective atmosphere, I did not foresee the problems that lay ahead of me . . .

I was very well looked after at mama's house. I made good friends with his daughters, Ragini and Radhika. But I missed Ma. I missed Rahul. I missed nanima. I missed home. This was all so new for me . . . to try and be independent, personally and professionally.

On the work front, I was learning new lessons too—in this industry, no one ever refuses you anything. People you approach will say yes sweetly and put you on hold indefinitely and then disappear, dangling you on your hopes. I feel that the reason for this behaviour is that they don't want to jeopardize any contacts—what if in this unpredictable profession a person who is a nobody now becomes super successful and that they have a need for that person in the future. Then at least they would be able to say that they had never refused that person in their earlier days.

So, to mark the beginning of my struggles in the film world, I made a list of people I wanted to meet. I borrowed the film directory from my nana and make calls every day to fix meetings with producers.

Everyone would meet me. Some out of courtesy, some because it was the norm and some, simply because they did not want to let pass an opportunity to meet a young and pretty girl! I was so naïve! I used to go to every production office with *mithai ka dabba*s, boxes of sweets that I'd got from Ludhiana as I didn't know how else to start a conversation than the typical Punjabi way of saying, '*Ji wo apke liye thodi mithai layi thi ghar se* (I'd got this small box of sweets from home for you).'

Ma would pack me so many of those dabbas when I visited her. Even now a few producers remember me as the newcomer with the 'mithai ka dabbas'.

I would meet them. Some would sign me up, some would ask me to come and meet them again, and some would say, 'We're still writing, we'll let you know...'

It was the world of vagueness. And I had newly arrived from the world of trust. So I happily called Ma, believing all of them, and told her that I had signed twenty films.

Obviously, she didn't believe me. Obviously, those films never started. Obviously, I kept waiting endlessly.

And kept hearing, 'We will let you know...'

It was exhausting and emotionally draining to meet those who weren't in the least bothered about me. I only had myself to look out for my interests. I used to miss my Ma. No one knows this but I would bite into the pillow and cry all night. Was it that tough to get a film? To realize your dream? I didn't know the answers then but I felt that I needed to get away from it all for a while. I decided to take a break and go home.

Next thing I knew, I'd boarded the train home and made my first journey alone. As the Ludhiana station was about to arrive, my heart started beating faster. This happiness was bigger than anything, to see Ma and Rahul! My world!

The train became slow as it neared the station and my eyes started looking for them. From the still moving train, I jumped out the moment

I saw her. And she held my hand! I laughed. But I cried more.

She knew something was not right. Mothers always do.

Back home, I spent each moment possible with Ma, played with Rahul, sat with nani and talked endlessly. Ma was making a mental note of everything. She saw I was happy, happy being home; yes, my roots were my strength.

As my return date drew closer, Ma asked me, 'You want to go back?'

I didn't say anything and I guess she got her answer. 'Okay, in that case, I am coming with you.'

Soon she and I were on the best train journey ever—singing, playing antakshri, befriending co-passengers, who, with Ma around, of course became like family members, getting off at stations and having *kulhad ki chai* and *pakoda*s (tea in earthen cups and fried snacks).

The journey of life with Ma, too, was so awesome. Every station of life, a beautiful landmark.

The train reached Mumbai with the two crazy women yet again. When I looked at Ma, I could not figure out what was really going on in her mind. But I was certain Dr Nalini Dutta had a gameplan for her daughter.

15

A Decision Is Made

§

Ma had decided to make me live independently, take my own decisions, make my own mistakes and learn from them, and be my own master!

Unless I was on my own, I wouldn't learn to fight the outside world. I had to walk my own path. I had to fall and I had to learn to get up and walk again. She shared her decision with the family too, and they all supported her. Mama and mami helped Ma look for a good place and a good manager for their niece who was going to start her own journey . . .

Before she returned to Punjab, it was all done. She bought me a beautiful one-bedroom house in Juhu, she hired a maid to take care of me 24 x 7 and bought me a car, a purple Maruti Zen, her favourite colour. She'd equipped me with all that I could need. She told me, '*Ab araam se struggle kar.*

Tera apna ghar, teri gaadi, sab hai tere paas (You have your own house, car, everything you need to lessen your struggle) and I am a phone call away.'

How easy she had made everything! I felt so lucky, so fortunate that I had a parent who was believing and investing in my dreams while putting a lot at stake. How many kids can say that their parents stood by them when they chose such a diverse profession?

My respect for Ma just increased manifold. What mattered for her was that Divya was happy. *Bas* (that's it). Nothing could come to conflict with that. She could and would stand and stop any *garam hawa* (warm wind) that blew my way.

Meri pyari si genie Ma . . . (my sweet genie-like Ma . . .)

It was soon time for her to leave for Punjab. She had set me up so well that suddenly I found a new confidence to be independent. It felt really nice to own my house, to feel responsible for myself. A novel feeling, but a beautiful one nevertheless. It gave me the enthusiasm to take on the world all over again.

My neighbours were Farah and Sajid Khan who had just started their careers too. So Ma being Ma, introduced us! Not that she knew them any better other than being an ardent fan of their aunts, Honey and Daisy Irani, who were big child stars of their time. She also got me acquainted with everyone in the neighbourhood. She made sure there were people to keep an eye out for me and that I was taken care of. And then, finally, when she felt assured that everything that needed to be done was done, she booked her return ticket.

'I'll keep coming, beta.' With those reassuring words, she was gone.

It was like someone took away the shade of an umbrella right off my head. How amazingly secure one feels when another person is more worried about you than you yourself and when you don't have to bother about anything at all because you are taken care of.

After she left, I kept meeting producers. They kept making vague promises and I continued to hope.

At this stage Ma's phone calls were like a tonic for me. After fighting with the world, that one phone call reinstated my energies.

With her, 'Sab theek ho jayega (Everything will be fine)', she made me feel secure.

I never understood any layered comments from people, even if there were plenty of hints from them to meet them anywhere other than the office. I did not pick up on those hints. The good thing about this industry is, at least in my experience, that even though there probably is a casting couch, no one is really forced into it. It's your choice. Yes. It's always your choice to say no, to ignore it, or to take it up.

Since I didn't have any godfathers or sugar daddies around the industry, I learnt by trial and error. There wasn't a director I hadn't met, an office I hadn't gone to.

Soon I was signed for two big films opposite big stars but replaced overnight by somebody else because of the recommendations of a big sugar daddy!

I was heartbroken. I was seeing too many manipulations too soon. How could people break promises? How could they lie so much? Why couldn't they say things the way they were meant to be said?

Ma's letters, containing poetry in them, held me in good stead in these times. Her poems were self-composed, encouraging me to move on, undeterred. I held them close, sitting in my one-bedroom flat, thinking of her and what I was doing in that world full of deception. 'Had I made a mistake? Was nani right? Should I have gone back?' Such thoughts crowded my mind.

I looked at the big Sai Baba picture on the wall. He was smiling . . .

Fortunately, in the next few months things started to work out. I did very commercial films like *Suraksha* with Sunil Shetty, *Agnisakshi* with Nana Patekar and *Veergati* with Salman Khan. I was soon known as a younger version of Manisha Koirala. People had now started to recognize me a bit.

When I went home, Ma would introduce me proudly to her acquaintances, 'My daughter is in movies . . .'

'*Acha? Kaunsi? Kya naam bataya? Humne to dekhi nai kabhi* (Really, which one? What is the name? We haven't seen it),' they would say.

I used to look at Ma and her expression stayed with me.

That expression said to those people, 'Wait for a few more years. Wait till you see more of her films. Wait till you know her name by heart and read about her it in the news headlines . . .'

She had the confidence in me that I didn't have in myself but it rubbed off on me.

Nothing was really going great for me. But I knew. Something, somehow would change it all. Because someone who loved me too much believed in me.

My parents on their wedding day

Me as a baby with Ma

Ma and I. One from the photo session done by
Dad in their hospital compound

Dad and I, at one of my birthday
parties. I'm flaunting the *ghagra-choli*
gifted by him

At Rahul's birthday celebration
after I returned to Punjab

Ma being awarded the best senior medical officer award
by the then Governor of Punjab, S.S. Ray

Ma being presented an award

Ma with her staff at her retirement ceremony

Actor Sunil Dutt at the launch of Ma's book, *Tanhaiyyan*

Ma striking her favourite bhangra pose

Me on the covers of Ma's books, *Tanhaiyyan* and *Qatra-qatra Zindagi*

The most memorable trip to Kerala with our supermom!

Us together. The travelling *jodi* in Durban

Ma not letting the wheelchair stop her from having fun
at Universal Studios Singapore

Ma on a buggy ride in Central Park, New York.
She, like a queen, loved buggy rides

Ma's most favourite day, Rahul's wedding . . . dance of sheer joy

When we brought Shweta home. The ecstatic *sasu ma*!

With the newest addition to our family

16

Relationships Are Tricky!

§

So what if Ma had let me come to Mumbai, nani was still looking for the right match for me. And this time Ma didn't want to displease her mother.

She called me and said, 'One of your nani's distant relative's son wants to meet. *Ek baar mil le. Nahin acha lage to mana kar dena beta* (Meet him once. If you don't like him, you can refuse him.)'

That sounded reassuring. I agreed reluctantly. The day I was to meet the 'boy', I had gone for a meeting and was late in getting home. It seemed he was in a hurry to meet me as my maid told me that he had arrived twenty minutes earlier. I told her to get him seated and to offer him *chai–nashta* (tea and snacks). I was hoping nani wasn't expecting me to make it myself and go with a tray of samosas and chai to meet him!

Anyway there were two entries to my flat, so I entered from the back door, quickly changed and went to meet the guy.

When I lay my eyes on him first, a feeling of disbelief swept over me. Then, the challenge was to use all my willpower to control my laughter. There sat in front of me a man who was a vision in maroon—maroon shoes, maroon velvet coat and he had brought a maroon rose for me!

Everything was colour-coordinated in full preparation for the rishta.

His first line was, '*Aap haan kahen to main Mummy ko phone karun* (If you say yes I will call Mummy).'

I had to bite my lower lip to control my laughter. I barely managed to respond, '*Pehle main apni Mummy ko phone kar lun, please?* (Can I call my mother first, please?)'

There was nothing to say. All I could do was laugh uncontrollably, which irritated both Ma and nani.

Of course, after that, nani was strictly told not to send any more rishtas.

'*Divya khud hi dhoond legi* (She will find someone for herself),' Ma said.

Well, er . . . I found and I lost.

I think what I looked for in my men or rather boys, as most of the guys I dated were younger than me, was my Dad or maybe that 'being taken care of' feeling. But either the guys were still settling down or were not so mature. It felt like they were looking for their mother in me. I had the pattern of attracting that type. I was like Saif Ali Khan's character from *Dil Chahta Hai*.

Every time I met someone, I thought, 'This is it!' My world would begin to revolve around the guy. Other things would take a back seat. I would become the *kushal grihani* (adept homemaker) type. But when the guy couldn't turn 'kushal (great)' it would have to end. Then my world would end too. I would take a while to re-emerge from break-ups. My world would stop. I would become disconnected, irritable, would lose my appetite and stop meeting my friends. I would have nothing to look forward to. Again, Ma would help me a lot to get over such phases.

'Why do you emotionally depend so much on someone that it becomes easy for anyone to break you like this?' she'd say. I would then get back on my feet and back into action. Back with a bang as they say. I would then do better work, try and achieve better fitness levels, have more zest and enthusiasm in life—until, of course, I found love again.

I appeared strong to the world but was very vulnerable in my relationships. Very vulnerable to the people I loved. So for those who really loved me, it was a blessing. But for those who were just looking for a strong woman to hold them, I was not the right person because sometimes, just sometimes, I needed to be held too. I needed to be child-like too.

Ma wasn't like that. She was always in control of her emotions and the situations. No one could use how she felt about them or how they felt about her against her. She refused quite a few proposals too, because her kids were her priority. We made her feel complete. She never ever thought of remarrying or having a companion though there were so many suitors ready to marry the lovely lady, if only she had said yes.

To cite an extreme case, once a bearded baba came to our house in Punjab donning the garb of a yogi. When I told Ma some babaji had come to meet her, she said, '*Bhaga de usko! Shadi karne aya hai mujhse*. (Shoo him off! He's come to marry me.)'

I was zapped! She was that straight. As it turned out, he was an ex-colleague of Ma and

Dad, a doctor who had been crazily in love with Ma since college days. But I guess the dear old man got a bit carried away in showing Ma that he would renounce the world because she had refused to marry him!

Ma hated drama of any kind so she just walked out and asked me to tell him to leave.

I always wonder, if I had been that strong regarding myself, like Ma, would my life have been different? Maybe it still can be. Because I'm sure, being an ardent Yash Chopra movies' fan, I can say someone out there is made for me . . .

17

A Big Change

§

Now that I had found a foothold in Mumbai, I was trying to get used to the big city, to films, to new people and newer lifestyles. I often felt disoriented and was missing Ma terribly. The number of phone calls to her increased.

Ma would be seeing her patients when her nurse would come and say, '*Choti behenji ka phone hai Mumbai se* (Young miss has called from Mumbai).'

She would drop everything to talk to me. If she would be sleeping and she'd get up with a jolt as soon as she heard, '*Chote bibiji ka phone!* (A call from young miss!)'

She knew I needed her badly and that I was trying to draw all the strength I could by just hearing her voice. She also knew she couldn't be physically present with me so she made sure we were in constant touch through phone calls. However, when the number of phone calls touched ten to fifteen a day, it became tough for even her to handle.

This time nani suggested to Ma, 'Why don't you take a long leave and stay with her for a few months? She needs you and you are restless too!'

Ma was overwhelmed to see this support coming from nani. But it wasn't surprising. After all, nani loved her two crazy girls and she knew very well that both were not doing fine without each other. Ma, for the first time, became a very obedient daughter and took a long leave.

She called me up and said, '*Main aarahi hun!* (I'm coming!)'

I had barely heard the full sentence when I jumped from the bed and on to my maid who thought I had lost the plot. I went out and shopped for Ma's favourite vegetables. I planned to cook her an elaborate meal! And then her favourite vanilla ice cream had to be bought too. I also thought of cleaning the house all over again . . . there was so much to do! Ma would come in a few hours. I couldn't hold my excitement.

I told nana too, that Ma was coming.

I reached the station way ahead of time.

I was crying! I was happy! I was ecstatic! The world seemed so beautiful!

We had an ecstatic reunion. In the cab home, I held on to her dupatta. Rahul, my dearest brother, was with her too. He was going to take admission in a medical college in Mumbai. I was thrilled to know that he would be with me from now on. No more staying alone, struggling alone. And the icing on the cake was that Ma would be with us for a few months. This was bliss!

I could not thank nani enough for giving Ma this brilliant idea to be with her daughter. I made a call to her. I heard her voice on the other side, 'Hello.'

There was a long pause and I could only say, 'Thank you, nanima. *Aap bahut acche ho* (You are wonderful)!'

There was a pause on the other side too.

I heard an overwhelmed voice say, '*Khush reh beta* (Be happy my child).'

The next few days were like a dream. No amount of heartbreaks and rejections at work bogged me down. I didn't even have to make any phone calls now. Ma was right next to me.

How important it is to be around family to keep your sanity intact when the world around you is trying to tear you apart. How good you feel when you enter the door of your house and see the smiling faces of your loved ones who don't judge you, who love you for who you are, who don't measure you up for how successful or unsuccessful you are, who just love you unconditionally!

I became less stressed about work too. Rahul had got admission in a leading medical college. Both us kids would come home to Ma who welcomed us with *garma–garam khana* (hot food). Just like good old times.

I wasn't scared of lustful men anymore. I was not discouraged by the nos I heard. I wasn't bogged down by the vagueness and unpredictability of the people in this industry. There was sheer positivity every day waiting for me at home.

I started meeting people at home too, as I knew Ma would be there with me. Ma was such a gracious hostess. Everyone who came home— magazine or newspaper editors, journalists, producers, actors—always left with a distinct fondness for Ma. Ma created a bond with them and they really started caring genuinely for me and Ma—a rishta that extended a little beyond their work with me. Yes, people saw me differently, not as a typically filmy girl.

'*Sweet aur* (and) *simple hai,*' they would say. I started getting decent work too. Good television offers came by and a few multi-starrers.

Rahul and I got busy but Ma now had a lot of free time at hand. She was not used to it. In Punjab she was pressed for time. Here, all she had to do was wait for us. Her leave was still for two more months. We suggested she take up some charitable job in a gurudwara close by.

She was instantly selected by the gurudwara charitable hospital. I think she had a knack. There was soon a long queue of patients outside her cabin. People would wait to meet her—and she loved this new feeling of working for charity and doing sewa.

Ma had a very peculiar habit. She spoke English and Punjabi very fluently but whenever someone spoke to her in Punjabi, her natural instinct would be to reply in English and if she was spoken to in English, fluent Punjabi would come out of her mouth. It was both weird and hilarious!

She sounded like a foreigner speaking in English with those who spoke in Punjabi and talking in desi Punjabi with those who spoke in fluent English. We could somehow never unearth the reason why she did this, but the patients understood her language as it was also coated with all the love and Punjabi warmth!

Two months just flew past. It was time for her to go back. But now she didn't want to go. She was settled with her kids and charity work. So nani suggested that she come back and complete the little time left for her retirement as people were missing her and then she would also come back with Ma to us in Mumbai. We unanimously agreed.

Ma went back to Punjab. The phone calls continued but not as many as I used to make as I had Rahul with me now, who was quite a support.

It was close to a year since I had started staying independently. I had a few more releases and a few TV shows like *Kadam* and *Shanno ki Shaadi*.

So at this time when Ma said, 'My daughter's in the movies,' people were familiar with my name. And my face. That, in a small town, was a big thing. When Ma was about to retire, everyone insisted I go from Mumbai to be with her. I am glad I went because otherwise I would have missed what I saw.

It was winter, cold and foggy. My train to Punjab was delayed. Ma's retirement function was at 11 a.m. and I felt horrible being still stuck in the train!

As soon as the train touched the platform I jumped out and rushed towards the waiting car. It looked like a shot straight out of a Hindi film—pushing people to make way, telling the driver to pick me from a less crowded place, with everyone staring at me first before familiarity dawned, '*Isko kahin dekha hai na* (We have seen her somewhere).'

I finally made it to Ma's event. There was a crowd of about 1000 people. Ma's employees, fellow doctors, nurses, patients, bosses, ex-bosses and everyone from Sahnewal! They all stood with garlands in their hands. As soon as they saw me arrive, everyone heaved a sigh of relief and the ceremony started. They all garlanded Ma one by one. The petite Doctor Nalini was soon covered till the face with those garlands. Then came the turn of the shawls. All the women came and wrapped shawls around her as a mark of respect.

I could see everyone standing there so respectfully for a woman who'd served them for more than thirty years. She was the woman to go to if anyone felt sick or if anything went wrong. She had stood by each of them.

She liked doing it. To be with people. For people. I sometimes wondered why she wasn't in politics. People loved her!

Her staff had collected money and gifted her a gold jewellery set. Ma was overwhelmed.

That was the place where I had grown up too. The same people I had seen as a kid, now older and grey-haired, stood there with folded hands for Ma. Thanking her for everything.

Nani sat in the front row, a proud mother. I could see she was getting very emotional too. Ma got up and made her farewell speech. Thanking each one, remembering everyone. She reminisced about her wonderful time there—that's where she had first arrived as a bride and begun her career and that's where her career and family had flourished. That's where her kids had grown up. That's where she had lost her husband. That's where the people had stood by her like family.

She had won the trophy of the best doctor in the state, was promoted as the civil surgeon in rural Ludhiana and had retired with everyone around her. Nothing could take away the love everyone felt for her. Rahul was the only one missing on that occasion as he had exams. Ma was taken home from the hospital with *band baja*, fanfare, in her official hospital jeep!

Like a queen she worked, like a queen she'd ruled people's hearts and like a queen she was retiring. I was so, so proud of her!

Now began the most exciting part for me. Packing up for Ma and nani . . . three generations, three petite women, three friends—all Mumbai-bound. To our dear Rahul who was waiting for us there.

Another phase had begun.

18

Don't Mess with Ma!

§

We were all back together in Mumbai now. Nalini, as my friends called Ma, had a knack for making friends with the strangest of strangers. People I would take ages to open up to, she would have made best friends in literally two minutes! By the time I'd come to the drawing room, mentally preparing myself to talk business with someone in a certain way, I would see Ma chatting about their family's well-being and whether they'd like to have her famous *aloo-tikki* or sandwiches. To refuse food was not a choice at all in her house.

If I whispered in her ear to let me talk about work, she'd effortlessly say aloud, 'Oh, that I've spoken about with them already. They'll address your concerns, don't worry!' Then she'd ask her new best friend, '*Haina?* (Isn't it?)'

And they would also nod along as if they had only come to have tikkis. The work talk was a mere formality. She made it that easy for me. It just amazed me to see the ease with which she made people comfortable.

'*Dance karke dikhaoon* (Should I show you my dance)?' she'd ask my friends when they would come home and they would, of course, readily agree to see her typical 1950s moves to any and every number; her moves would loyally be the same—repeated yet thoroughly entertaining.

I had been guided by her in my film *Train to Pakistan*. The rolling of eyes, the fluttering of eyelids—I could never have done it with that ease had I not seen it being performed at home every evening with equal vigour by my very own Madhubala!

On the other extreme, with the same effortlessness with which she made friends, she could also shoo off anyone who dared to say anything unpleasant to her kids. One such incident happened very long ago. We used to go to Delhi by train to visit our buas during our school vacations. Ma's hospital was right next to the small railway station of Sahnewal, so her impressive entourage would very efficiently push all three of us into the non-reserved compartment!

In the overcrowded compartment, she had managed to plonk Rahul on someone's lap and got me half a seat with a lady. The lady wasn't the best of human beings I guess and she pushed me off the seat very rudely. Our co-passengers were trying to talk to her when my glance rested on Ma. She had a cold stare on her face. The subject of her attention was the lady. It was like a lull before the storm. I knew something dramatic was going to happen and I didn't have to wait too long for it. Ma lifted the woman off her seat and pushed her towards the co-passengers.

'How dare you hurt the kid?' she roared.

The woman now became meek and looked around for support but the public sympathy was with us. Ma made me sit again. I got my throne back. No one said anything.

A miracle had taken place—there was pin-drop silence in a second-class unreserved compartment of an Indian train. Ma had a protective smile on.

I, of course, didn't know where to look. One thing I knew well was that she was never to be crossed paths with. She was the firebrand Nalini.

If anyone took *panga* with me, I could easily have warned them with this famous dialogue from the hit Hindi film *Deewar*—'*Mere paas Ma hai* (I have my mother)!'

19

One Special Birthday

§

Ma never showed the need to have a friend, or a social circle, or maybe a kitty party group, neither in Mumbai nor in Sahnewal. Not that she had much of a choice in Sahnewal. There were not many women to match her sensibilities in that place. They were basically simple people, good enough to just to say hi and hello, not to pour your heart out to. For that she only had me, nani, Rahul and her writings. Yes, she used to write and write beautifully. Prose and poetry both. That was her outlet. Putting her loneliness on pieces of paper and crumpling them and throwing them into the bin, just like her emotions.

As kids in Sahnewal, Rahul and I watched that scene only from a distance because we were scared to ask why she threw away all that she wrote. Then we discreetly started taking those pieces out of the dustbin. My little brother was always very meticulous. He, in a very organized manner, compiled those crumpled pieces and put them away in a file, one by one.

Once, as was our daily routine, Ma, Rahul and I were up on the terrace, dancing. Ma went away after a while. We both kept dancing but she didn't come back. I came down looking for her but she was not to be seen anywhere.

Suddenly, I heard some sounds coming from under the bed. There she was, curled up like a baby, with a pen in her hand, tears in her eyes, hiding from the world and us. She was writing. Pouring her heart out about how she missed her husband, maybe feeling the vacuum a lot more than usual.

I didn't have the strength to pull her out. I just sat there, waiting there for her to come out.

Years later in Mumbai, I had fairly established myself as an actress, or can one ever say that in this insecure unpredictable field; I had a bit of a foothold, let's say. Ma's birthday was coming up and Rahul and I were wondering what gift would be ideal for this sweetheart of a mom. We started off deciding on a salwar–kameez, then changed it to a watch, instantly realizing these gifts were very impersonal. Suddenly, we both looked at each other and said, 'Should we get Ma's book published?'

Yes! That was the answer. It would be ideal if she had all her writings as a book. We knew it would give her great pleasure. However, we had no experience in book publishing. We didn't know where to start from. All we had was the intent.

To add to that, we were planning a surprise. '*Ma ko nahi batana hai* (We won't tell Ma).'

To start with, we opened the files and started reading the poetry. Both of us were crying. Nalini had gone through so much in her life! She had never let any hardship come even close to us. We had lived a royal life. She had borne all her storms alone. Maybe holding my little hand as a support sometimes but I wasn't aware of what she was going through inside.

I was reading it now. Those words were magical, beautifully woven, and straight from the heart.

Her journey alone. *Tanhaiyyan* (Loneliness) is what we titled her first poetry book.

She had particularly loved one of my black and white portraits. That became the cover picture. Rahul's friends came on board to print and publish the book.

Then we were left with the task of having a super event to release the book. The date, of course, was easy to decide. Her birthday, 20 December. The venue was her favourite ISKCON hall. She loved their food and ambience. Another major decision was choosing the chief guest. By now Rahul and I were too nervous to keep it a secret and we finally told Ma. She got so nervous that instead of giving us *shabashi* (kudos) we got a scolding. *Sweet wali*, of course! So now the three of us together pondered over names.

After a lot of brainstorming, I called him up. Ma had always been his admirer and more so after his march during the terror days in Punjab— Mr Sunil Dutt, one of the finest human being I have known. He picked up the phone himself. I nervously greeted him and told him about our plans for Ma's birthday and invited him. Not as an actor but as a child requesting his presence.

'*Main aawanga pucca* (I will definitely come)', he said in Punjabi.

He made it all sound so easy that I couldn't believe it even after it was done!

'Should I call him again? Should I re-confirm? What if he was just sweet to me? What if he forgets? Should I remind him?'

I hardly slept during the next ten days. It wasn't just another function. It was Ma's birthday, after all! It was her book launch. It had to be special. We had invited all the people we knew, done what we could have. We only had to wait now.

Finally, the day arrived. It was Ma's birthday and none of us were smiling. We were nervous as hell. Rahul and I were trying to paste on fake smiles, but Ma wasn't even trying! She was nervous and grumpy!

'*Kya tension de di birthday pe! Kahin chota mota dinner kar aate bas* (Why have you given me so much tension on my birthday! We could have just gone for a small dinner somewhere)!'

On top of that we had asked her to prepare a speech.

She snapped, 'I don't *prepare* speeches! All my life, I've spoken impromptu!'

The event was at 6 p.m. The three of us were at the venue at 4 p.m. Sipping water, setting chairs, making calls, looking expectantly at the gate. Praying. Yes! Praying, that all goes well.

At 5.45 p.m., my friends started coming in. Then Ma's friends came. But the hall still looked empty like the venue of '*ghar ka birthday party*' (a regular birthday party at home).

I just wanted to run away.

I so badly wanted this evening to be special! I could see my mother smiling and chatting with someone, simultaneously looking at the clock. It was ten minutes to 6 p.m.

A friend had set up Ma's books on a table for sale.

Ma said, '*Log ayenge to khareendenge na* (Only if people come they will buy)!'

I wish I had a magic wand!

Maybe someone up there heard me. Within five minutes, things changed. The press and media arrived, so did lots of other guests.

At sharp 6 p.m. I could hear the siren and Ma, Rahul and I ran out! It was Sunil Duttji! He had kept his promise to his doctor saheba. The place was now flooded with people.

Sonu Nigam, my bestie, came and made the inaugural speech and invited Ma on stage. Rahul and I were holding hands.

Dutt saheb spoke about Ma. He knew a lot about her. It was turning out to be such a lovely birthday for her. Those words he spoke were so amazing and encouraging. I read excerpts from the book and everyone was cheering Ma.

I looked around. All the leading directors, editors and actors were there! Those who didn't know me very well too were in attendance; this show of support was really touching. In an industry which is need-driven, this was an amazing gesture for a mother, celebrating her journey . . .

Then, Ma spoke. Yes, impromptu. She was all heart. There was pin-drop silence. Everyone listened intently to every word she said. After a few nervous seconds initially, she seemed to enjoy it, the natural that she was. She peppered her speech with anecdotes and poetry. The audience loved it as did she.

And her kids? We could have cried out of sheer happiness. To see her play a new role on her birthday. Of collecting the pages of her life and giving her a title—poetess!

After the event got over and Dutt saheb left, we finally relaxed and smiled. Rahul and I went to the table where Ma was signing copies of her book.

She was getting mobbed!

In that noise, we both heard ourselves mumble, 'Happy birthday, Ma.'

20

'Divya ki Mummy'—
The Unconventional Star Mom!

§

Films are so unpredictable. You never know if you belong in one and until you start a project, there's a tension and lingering uncertainty which can be very disorienting.

To go a little back in time, I had just wrapped up *Train to Pakistan* and had been signed up for Gurdas Maan's *Shaheed-e-Mohabbat*. Gurdas Maan's wife, Manjit Maan, who was the producer of the film had seen *Train to Pakistan* and was keen to cast only me as the lead!

As Ma was posted as a civil surgeon in Ludhiana and I was to shoot in Chandigarh, Ma took leave and joined me. A day passed, and then two. But I had not been called on the set. After three days when Ma and I were taking a walk outside the circuit house in Chandigarh where the unit was staying, I voiced aloud my apprehension to her, 'Ma why are they not calling me for the shoot? Did they get someone else? Are they not telling us?'

But Ma was positive and patient, 'Wait, beta . . . *kal dekhthte hain* (let's wait till tomorrow).'

And they did call me the next day. I started shooting.

Ma was with me throughout most of my shootings, regardless of whether they were fun or tough shoots. Her chair was always placed on the set. Watching over me, but also befriending everyone from the spot boy to the director.

'*Divya ki mummy*' (Divya's mom), she was fondly called.

I remember once we were in Rajasthan in the biting cold of the Jaisalmer dunes. No vanity vans could go after a point and we were shooting at night. The temperature had dropped to -5 degrees. Ma insisted she'd come with the unit, which comprised only about fifteen people, to look after her daughter. She carried a bottle of brandy to rub on my hands in case I felt very cold. She was very confident she'd manage. No chair could be kept for her on the dunes so my spot boy spread a mattress for her to rest on. In between my shots, I'd exchange glances with her and she'd smile back or I would go to her and she'd rub brandy on my hands.

After a bit, it became very cold. I saw Ma had covered herself with the mattress she sat on. The director called me for the shot and the song was played on the recorder.

On the dunes, on that biting cold night, the song sounded mesmerizing. As the shot got cut, I looked for Ma and saw she had befriended a camel guy and was sitting next to the fire he had lit! She signalled me to come too, but the director called me again. After I was done with the shot I looked for her again and I was startled. She was not to be seen!

'Where could she have disappeared amidst the dunes?' I wondered. My heart skipped a thousand beats.

I asked my spot boy, '*Ma kahan hain* (Where is my mother)?' He also looked around frantically and then he smiled and pointed out.

There . . . far away, tucked in the thick blanket of camel skin, were two faces, one of the camel guy and the other, my mother's.

A smile came on my face. She was gesturing again . . . to me to rub the remaining brandy on my hands.

Another kind of warmth filled my heart. It still does, whenever I think of my adorable Mummy on the sets with me.

21

A Trip to Pakistan

§

Travels around the world with Ma consist of some of my fondest memories with her. And the best of them all was taking her back to her birth place, Karachi.

I had heard so many Partition stories from her, about how she was just four when they had to leave the huge haveli they lived in, travelling on empty stomachs for days. At the railway station, someone had dropped a *matthi* (a fried snack). Seeing that, my mother, little Nalini, left her mother's hand to go pick it up. But before she could get to it, her mother had hurriedly carried her away to catch the train to Delhi, her eyes still on the matthi . . .

That's the reason Ma never let us waste anything, ever.

'*Khaane ki kadar kiya karo* (Respect food)!' she'd always say.

So, when I got an offer to act in a Pakistani series in Karachi post my film, *Veer–Zaara*, I lapped it up, mostly for this reason that Ma was born there.

Ma and I got a warm welcome in Karachi. *Veer–Zaara*'s Shabbo was a hot favourite there. So everyone was very eager to show us around.

The first place we wanted to look for, though we weren't sure if it would still be around, was the haveli that was Ma's home. Ma's memory as a four-year-old was still fresh. She gave visual details of the area as much as she could and the people there really made an effort to find out. Finally, we got to know that there was indeed a place matching Ma's description. We went there. I stood behind and let Ma explore the place on her own. A lot had changed but a lot had remained the same too. She slowly went around, absorbing the atmosphere ... She stopped at the *chaukhat* (entrance) of an old haveli. Minutes passed by and then she came back to me.

'*Bhookh lagi hai* (I'm hungry),' is all she said. We didn't talk. We didn't need to. I could see the glint in in her eyes. On our way back, she hugged me tight, 'You re-introduced me to my childhood. Thank you, beta!' I had a lump in my throat. There couldn't be a more beautiful feeling than to see your parent that happy.

The shooting was going on smoothly too and the producer had become my mother's *mooh bola beta* (a foster child by promise) by then! He decided that my mother had to do a lucky mascot 'guest appearance' role in the series for him. Ma refused initially but she didn't require much convincing. Her childhood's best actor trophies were calling out to her and she bragged a bit in front of her newly acquired son. He became more insistent that Mummyji had to play the role of a doctor who visits me.

I was very amused but I encouraged her too. She put on the greasepaint and was all set to share screen space with her daughter. All she had to do was check my blood pressure and write some medicines but what she kept doing instead was prescribing the medicines first and then checking the blood pressure. After about twenty retakes, the producer decided that he had rubbed enough good luck into this series! And Ma decided that she was a better doctor in real life than the reel one and that he hadn't been fair to make her play herself and not enact a dramatic role instead. They promised to collaborate on a future project soon.

I was just giggling away seeing this display of love. There was a lot of warmth and affection which I could feel clearly. Ma had that knack of making people her own.

Soon I pulled my lovely doctor saheba away from the crowd to go look up her city with her. Travelling with her was so rejuvenating. She wanted to see every nook and corner of where she was born, where little Nalini had played, where all the memories lay . . .

She was like this little girl and I like her Ma, holding her finger taking her through the lanes of her childhood . . .

22

Around the World
with Pari Maa

§

Ma, Rahul and I were partners in seeing the world. Because of his clinic, Rahul used to join us occasionally but most of the time it was only Ma and I travelling together. Whoever booked my tickets for events, awards or my shoot knew Nalini Dutta was my travel companion, always.

She was my best friend and the most entertaining companion. She loved seeing places. She wasn't the typical tourist who likes to go shopping. She liked to absorb the ambience of a place.

I remember we had gone to Amsterdam for three days for the IIFA awards. Everyone was either jet lagged or resting after reaching there.

I too had plonked myself on the bed.

Ma patted me on my back, '*Chal uth, chai banati hun* (Get up, I'll make tea), then we'll go see the city!'

She surprised me with her enthusiasm and zest for life. A cup of black tea was all she needed to get rejuvenated. So soon, hand in hand, we were out on a bus ride seeing and exploring the city—churches, museums, city-rides, restaurants. And then we went to the famous red-light area of Amsterdam. We were very intrigued by the culture there. What both of us didn't know was that one was not supposed to take photographs there. The ignorant tourists that we were, we started doing just that and before I knew it, one of the girls was chasing me. Ma and I ran from there, first for our dear lives, and then giggling like two naughty girls . . .

I never felt she was just my Ma. She was my friend—best friend, in fact.

Paris, London, Dubai, US, Durban, Singapore . . . were some very memorable trips with her. She had enjoyed each moment. And her enjoyment was infectious too.

You would never see her behave like an elderly person and say, 'My joints are paining, *betaji aap jao* (you go my child).' Instead she said, 'I definitely have to go and visit this place. You may stay back if you like!'

The most memorable trip was when she had just come out of a paralytic stroke on her left side. I remember we had had a terrible time coping with it until she got slightly better and Rahul, with his acupuncture, got her back on her two feet. Her left side was still weak but she made an effort to walk. All three of us had become so mentally exhausted that the moment Ma was better, we went for a mini-break to the Kerala backwaters. We'd booked a houseboat in Alleppey. Rahul and I decided to look up the small villages there in a small canoe but for that one had to leave the houseboat and jump into the canoe. We were all set, but there was a small issue.

Ma also wanted to come. In that condition, there was the danger of her injuring herself again if she were to jump into the canoe. No elderly person would have even thought of this. But she had a brilliant idea.

'I'll stand on the houseboat. You hold me and then lower me. They'll catch me from the canoe. I'm sure they are very efficient people!'

We looked at her in disbelief. She had no fear of how she would physically manage to get on the canoe but her child-like excitement to enjoy something was so strong that everything else took a back seat and everyone had to relent.

The 'mission Nalini' was completed successfully. Our hearts were literally in our mouths when she was being shifted.

But she was smiling, '*Life enjoy karo, yaar* (Enjoy your life!)!' she said with the enthusiasm of a teenager. And we did! We stopped by different villages in that canoe and had *nariyal* pani (coconut water) while dipping our feet in the water. As the canoe sailed along more villages, we picked up food from the villagers.

It was amazing and as an afterthought, it would not have been half the fun had Ma not been with us.

Generally while travelling, Mom would be the most excited to see the menu on the flights. She loved being pampered and such was her presence that people loved pampering her too. The hostesses would keep coming back to her, 'Aunty, another glass of juice?'

She'd look at me for permission as if I was her mum!

On one such travel we were on our way back from Hong Kong. Ma was eating and watching the film, *Gangs of Wasseypur* on the flight. The rest of the gang with us, Shah Rukh Khan, Anupam Kher, Shahid Kapur and Javed Akhtar saheb decided to play dumb charades. So Ma's side of the aisle was chosen to enact the name of the movie. Now, some of them being actors, they would get really animated. And every time they would accidentally press Ma's movie screen! Poor Ma, she had to see the same scene of the film at least five times. Of course, she would have killed me with her expression had it been me doing that. However, she couldn't really say much when Shah Rukh said, 'Sorry, Aunty,' with his disarming smile.

'*Koi baat nai beta, aur khelo* (No issues son, keep on playing)!' she chirped.

'Yeah, right!' I thought. All this because of Shah Rukh's smile! She would not have made that concession for me!

Before alighting, her wheelchair was pulled into the aircraft as the distance till the arrival gate was too far.

She said, 'Everyone's looking at us. *Wo kya sochenge, Nalini wheelchair mei ja rahi hai* (What will they think, Nalini is going on a wheelchair)! Then how will I be Shah Rukh's girlfriend?' she joked.

In spite of my protestations, she said assertively, 'I am going to walk myself, beta.' Smiling disarmingly at everyone even though she was a bit tired because of her weak leg and a bit breathless because of her heart—but no one could make that out. She walked fast like a delightful young girl, waving out at Anupam Kher and Shah Rukh who were waving back at her.

Like a little baby. Yes, I had a little daughter and I had named her 'Pari . . . Pari Maa'. That's what I called her always.

23

Stage and Appearances!

How much ever confident and strong I might look, there's always a nervousness that strikes me before a live event. Some say it's good to have nervous energy on stage. Thankfully, the nervousness lasts only till I reach the stage. Once I am on the stage, I feel I own it. But the time before that is hell for me and people close to me. Especially for Ma.

My nervousness starts a day before the event ...

I would write my lines, borrow *shero-shayari*, poetry, from Ma, discuss with her, rehearse, go about doing other preparations. But I would have palpitations, which only Ma would see. Hence I would sometimes get cranky or snap at her with, 'Lemme work, Ma!'

She would quietly sit with me, pat my head and read her paper. Her mere presence soothed my spirits quite a bit. After rehearsing all I could, Ma would put my head on her shoulder and say, 'Shut your eyes for ten minutes and relax, you've been working too hard.'

I would resist even though I would be dying to rest my head on Ma's arm . . . and I would lie down quietly. She would then pat my head, sing me a lullaby. Yes, we extended our lullaby sessions by more than a few years. I would instantly doze off to la la land. In exactly twenty minutes she would wake me up with a steaming cup of chai.

'*Chal uth* (Get up)! Get ready now!'

How could I not be totally and absolutely in love with this adorable woman! Power nap followed by a potent cup of cardamom–ginger tea, I used to feel absolutely fresh and energetic to go for the show, palpitations still there!

In most cases, I took Ma along with me as I could barely handle myself before going on stage. Only she could. She had the most important role of holding my hand! Rahul often made fun of this. 'When will you grow up, Divu?' he would say teasingly.

He was right though. The world outside thought that they were dealing with the strongest woman they had come across, an accomplished actor, who didn't even need a paper to do her job superbly well on stage.

That might be the case on stage, to an extent. But till the moment I would get up there, I was a bundle of nerves. However, no one would know except my mother.

The organizers would make a zillion last minute changes in the show and I would super-confidently take them into account and help them plan the show. They would never make out that while my right hand wrote the notes with ease, my left was holding Ma's hand tightly. It gave me the most reassuring feeling that all was well, that everything would turn out positively, and that she was around. And that after the show went smoothly, she and I would go out and have dinner.

Her reassurances would continue until she had to say bye to me at the first step of the stage! Until then I would have taken hundreds of good luck wishes, kisses and hugs from her. Once on the stage, a warm feeling of owning it ensued and from there on I felt at home exchanging happy glances with Ma sitting in the audience.

In the applauses and cheers from the audience, I'm sure somewhere, looking at the finally happy and relieved me, Ma would have been very amused too, with her child who exuded so much confidence on stage but at the same time needed confidence from her mother and derived it from her in those small, beautiful, reassuring ways . . .

24

Happiness of a Wedding . . .

§

Seeing the unpredictability of my life and profession, the '*shadi ka bhaar* (the onus of getting married)' had now fallen on my sibling, *chote bhaiya* Rahul! It had always been like that in our house. When I had decided to be an actor and eventually could not find my Mr Right at the so called right time, everyone looked hopefully at poor Rahul to carry on the family baton. He had no choice but to agree.

Rahul, my dear brother, did date a few girls but his marriage was a traditional affair. Even though I was incredulous about this process, he sat with Ma to find rishtas on Shadi.com. They would often force me to sit with them and check out profiles of girls I liked.

It was amazing. Despite many misses, one day Rahul walked into my room and said, 'So I've liked a girl and am going to meet her in Delhi.'

I thought it was going to be another date with a girl he would ultimately reject but he called me and Ma from Delhi soon after meeting her.

'Ma, I like her, you can go ahead with talking to her parents,' he said, clearly happy. Ma and I were very happy too, but it also hit us how things would change from then on. A new member was going to join our family.

They say sons change post marriage. Ma did feel a bit insecure. So did I, but I guess it's more of a mother–son thing. Though Ma has been the most liberal-minded woman I've known and more of our friend, when it came to having to share her son, even though briefly, a sadness hit her. Ma and I sat down at our favourite spot by the window, as we often did to discuss all our issues, over tumblers of chai. So Rahul had grown up— we let the thought sink in. He was on the verge of starting a new life.

'Will he live separately now, Ma?' my voice cracked as I asked her. 'Will things change now?'

Ma kept looking outside and then having finally come upon a decision said, 'No, we will all live together. The four of us.' She called up Rahul and asked him if he and his fiancée would be okay to stay on with us. He was happy with Ma's decision. Somehow, the three of us just didn't know how to live without each other. An addition to the family was great as long as she joined the group.

The preparations for the marriage started in full swing. Once Ma was assured of the family only growing, she was unstoppable. She wanted the best for her *bahurani*, her would-be daughter-in-law. Purchasing the wedding ring took the longest time. Ma, Rahul and I had probably visited and revisited all the jewellers in town. Even the staff at the jewellers began to recognize my brother after a while. I teased both of them, saying that he must have been the most excited *dulha* (groom) and Ma, the most excited *saas* (mother-in-law).

If they had their way, they would have started dancing even in the shops!

There was extreme happiness around our household at that time. I hadn't seen any of us being so happy ever before. Friends and relatives joined in the festivities too! Every day was a celebration. At Rahul's mehendi ceremony the three of us applied mehendi together and danced vigorously to loud music.

Memories from the past, of the three of us together, flashed in front of my eyes: the little Rahul who piggy-backed on me, the blind man's bluff games, school trips, summer vacations, family holidays, pranks, our alone times, the fun times and the tough times—everything! I went and kissed Rahul. 'He would really make a very handsome *dulha*,' I thought at that moment.

The wedding day was hectic. No matter how well prepared one is, something or the other needs to be done at the last minute. In all the running around here and there, pundits, parlours, people . . . we didn't get to know when it was time for the *baraat* (marriage procession).

I will never forget this scene: Ma was in front of the horse on which her son was sitting with a *sehra* (a curtain of flowers) covering his face. It had been her dream to see her son like that. She kept looking at him and smiling and dancing. Yes, she was the happiest that day!

Absolutely glowing!

I've always wondered if people are embarrassed to dance in a baraat as the procession winds down the road. I being an actor had double the reason to be hesitant. But once the dhol started, and the friends and family pulled Ma on the floor in front of the horse, there was no stopping us, the two Punjabi ladies. The crazy two had gotten together after a long time to dance on a very special occasion!

With lots of *dhol-dhamaka*, the bride was brought home. By that time everyone in the marriage party was exhausted. Hindu weddings go on till very late in the night. All the cute ceremonies with the bride and groom were performed. Rahul let the bride win most of the games, much to the displeasure of the girls at home! But at that moment he was a very happy man.

～

The reception day saw me and my cousins run to the venue at least five times. We were just not satisfied! I changed the menu, the decor, everything, thrice! Thank God, the wedding contractors were my ardent fans or I am sure they would have told me to take a chill pill. But it was my kid brother's wedding and the entire industry was invited. I was very nervous. I'd just come back home to change when I realized that the wedding invitation said 7 p.m. instead of 8 p.m. I got extremely irritated because as hosts we would now have to sit there from 7 p.m. onwards even though it was hardly likely that anyone would turn up that early.

Er . . . I was wrong! There are some punctual people left in this world!

I saw Mr Prem Chopra arrive with his wife. Mom was still at home getting ready! She was usually the person at the foreground when it came to chatting up with people. I looked around. The bride and the groom were busy clicking pictures in extremely funny poses from the 1950s. I didn't want to disturb them, but Prem uncle was extremely fond of Rahul. Rahul had medically treated him on many occasions. So the bride and groom came to meet them. There was an awkward moment amongst us. Pictures were clicked to fill that awkward space; they promised to return and left. I wasn't even fully dressed. My Riyaz Gangji jacket lay on chair. I quickly wore it before the wrong time on the cards embarrassed me again.

I wanted Ma to come as soon as possible as she was a pro at making conversations. She finally arrived, looking stunning in beige with a signature rose in her hair and a bright smile. She didn't even bother to inspect the venue I had so painstakingly chosen, readied and then got redone. She was in her own world . . . made of bliss.

Rahul introduced her to a couple asking, 'Remember them, Ma?'

Ma very enthusiastically responded, 'Of course', and got into an animated discussion with them for about twenty minutes. I butted in to take Ma away to meet someone else and on our way there, I inquired who she was talking to.

'I have no idea!' she said.

'So how did you chat with them then and make it seem as if you'd known them for years! *Kamaal ho* (You're amazing)!'

And we both giggled and took our first drink to raise a toast to the man of the house! Yes, that day, the son of the house had been promoted!

At about 9 p.m., the who's who of the film industry started arriving, so did our friends and family and our folks from Punjab.

It was great to see everyone come together after so long to wish Rahul and Shweta, Nalini's son and daughter-in-law. They had to be there. Nalini had left a mark in their lives in some way or the other. Even if it wasn't her business. Getting someone a job, sorting someone's marital problems, just hearing somebody out, sending her signature *kadhi–chawal* and *tikki* to someone's house or just spending quality time with them, Ma had a way with people . . . right into their hearts. And they were all present to be with her on her special day. *Ek laute bete ki shadi* (Her only son's wedding)! Yes, it was a memorable night.

Slowly, all the guests left one by one. In earlier times, after our parties, the three of us would sit down to chill, assess the party, gossip and have fun. We were about to do the same now when we realized there was a new member in our group who was here to stay now and she was looking at me and Ma. The gossip and the fun went out of the window and we both became prim and propah. Rahul and Shweta stood in front of Ma to take her blessings! Ma didn't know what was to be said after they'd touched her feet. So she helplessly looked at me. I was biting my dupatta trying to control my laughter. Soon the lovely girl would find out that her mother-in-law did not expect her to touch her feet at all! Rather she wanted to be friends and have a cup of chai in her steel tumbler with her! Rahul made the funniest picture, sandwiched as he was between what he was used to doing with the crazy women at home and what was expected of him as a newly married husband. In his entire life, this was probably the first time he'd touched Ma's feet. He normally would have hugged her, kissed her, lifted her in his arms! Everything but that.

Gradually, Shweta realized that there was an ease about our household. No rules. No norms. But yes, Ma's was the final word!

We, the three of us now, had come to terms with that.

25

The Two-minute Magic

§

Ma was a two-minute chef! Literally! She could give Maggi a run for their money! When she said she would make something in two minutes, she meant exactly that! And she made it deliciously well. I have no idea where she picked her cooking skills from because all she really knew before coming to live with me in Mumbai was to cook parantha and chai. Very well at that! When she came to Mumbai, she started cooking with a lot of interest. And she had Punjabi *jadu* (magic) in her hands.

She used to never measure masalas. *Bas*, she would take the powders in her hand and without even looking at the quantity, throw them into the frying pan, stir whatever she was making and it would be done in no time.

'In two minutes,' she would say. '*Bas*, ready to serve . . .'

It would shock many. How was it even possible? they would wonder.

When we would visit someone's house and they would take a while to get chai ready, Ma would get restless. She would also be very curious about what people do in the kitchen for so long! My poor bhabhi, Shweta, had just been welcomed into the house and she was to make her first token lunch! After she saw the pace at which Ma cooked, she looked at me, and I returned her helpless look back with a 'I understand!' When it was her turn, she was following recipes meticulously and Ma was impatiently looking at her slow but exact movements. My job was to keep gesturing to Mom to be patient with other people's cooking. Rahul's job was to ensure that his bride didn't drop the food or utensils or herself out of sheer nervousness! Anyway . . . Rahul and I were successful! Ma was patient and Shweta didn't fall! The food was yummy but, of course, the time taken wasn't close to two minutes. The lovely bride made her mark in Ma's good books for cooking a delicious meal but with a remark, 'Timing needs to be better!'

Ma loved to invite people home. Once Ma, along with me and a couple of my friends, were coming back from a play. I was shooting for a

Shyam Benegal film the next day and had big dialogues to mug up. So I was in a hurry to get home! I asked my friends if they would like to grab a few rolls on the way before we split. But Ma, being Ma, kept insisting we go home for dinner. 'I'll make it in two minutes and then you guys can go,' she said. I wanted to nudge her to remind her that I had a shoot to prepare for but she looked at everyone but me because she knew I would stop her. My friends could not say no to Ma and they looked at me for an invitation. I had to also give in! How would she be able to prepare a proper dinner in two minutes, I wondered!

As we entered home she asked me to spread a mat on the bed, set the plates and chat with my friends. I had specific instructions not to disturb her at all in the kitchen! I had just started cribbing to my friends about the long dialogues I had to learn when Ma pushed open the bedroom door! In one hand she had steaming hot paranthas, in the other, a kadai with pulao she had made out of the boiled rice in the fridge. She exited only to re-enter with her signature *jeera aloo sabji* and *aam ka achar*. In literally a few minutes, the entire spread was laid. We squatted on the bed as Ma put the food on everyone's plates. I had forgotten all my tension about the shoot and the dialogues. What I could only see and absorb was the delightful aroma of Ma's food served with so much love and warmth. I just lovingly looked at Ma. She had literally fought with me to bring my friends home. And I am glad she did. They were glad she did . . .

As they took her leave they said, 'Aunty, we have never had such a delicious meal and you made it in two minutes! *Aaj neend achi ayegi* (We will sleep well tonight)!'

To have a Ma like that . . . *Mujhe bhi* (I will too).

26

The Last Days

This chapter is going to be the most difficult one to pen down, Ma. I have picked up the pen to write many times and kept it down again. I didn't have the heart to or maybe wasn't mentally prepared to relive the trauma. Ever again.

Denial was better.

Her heart problem had always been an issue. But she had never let it bog her down or used her health as a reason to not accompany me somewhere. She'd just pop a pill, put on her best clothes and her smile, hold my hand and go out with me.

But it was an issue. Her heart. She had had many angioplasties earlier and we knew this time it would have to be a bypass, something we all dreaded.

I was shooting the climax of *Chalk and Duster* with Shabana Azmi, Rishi Kapoor and

Juhi Chawla, when I got a call. I knew from the tone of Rahul's voice that Ma wasn't well.

I always panicked when Ma fell ill, this time even more so. My palms began to sweat and I was finding it difficult to breathe. I just wanted to rush home to Ma. Everyone noticed that and enquired after me. Shabanaji and Rishi Kapoorji were very reassuring, 'Go to the best surgeon, get it sorted.'

That was my biggest fear. Ma didn't want to get a bypass done. Neither did we want her to. Something about it petrified us.

Juhi told me, 'Take your mom to a health farm; one gets totally lost in these hospitals.' She was speaking from experience, as her brother had been comatose in a hospital for months.

I just wanted to go home, see her hale, hearty and smiling. I wanted to get her dressed and go out with her, hand in hand.

However, when I got home, it was all quiet. Ma was resting. Rahul took me to another room and said, 'She's agreed to a bypass and we'll get the best surgeon, don't worry!'

We had no choice. This lady in the next room was my lifeline! I couldn't imagine life without her. Not for a moment. She had to get better.

Soon we consulted a top surgeon and a date was locked for the bypass.

Everything happened very quickly from then on. Friends and family visited to wish Ma all the best. Ma was nervous.

Like a baby, she sat on my lap, '*Divu, main theek ho jaaongi na, yaar* (I will get okay, no?)?' she asked.

I bit my lip to hold back my tears and be the strong mother to her that she had been for me.

'Yes, of course, Gudiya, there's no other way. We'll get through it together. You'll be fine!'

Ma's surgery was done and she came home hale and hearty until her stitches caught an infection and her doctor gave the infection more time than it required, to heal. That, for Ma, and for us, was the most difficult time. To see her writhing in pain, waiting for the infection to heal.

Listening helplessly to the doctors' reassurances, taking her from one hospital to the other for check-ups, holding her hand, watching her suffer . . . it was all too much. I couldn't bear to see her even cough; to see her suffer so much in pain was like dying a thousand deaths.

We did what we could, running to those busy doctors, wondering why the wound was getting worse . . .

Ma was in hospital again for a clean-up. It was a minor thing, we thought. After that she'd be fine and she'd come home.

As I wheeled her in, she held my hand and cried for the first time like a baby! I wondered why, but I guess she knew better . . .

That night I stayed with her in the room, looking after her. She was in pain and I just couldn't bear to see her like that.

'*Khush reh mera bachcha* (Be happy, my child), you are a very good kid,' she mumbled.

The next day her condition deteriorated. The doctors had to put her in the ICU. She wasn't eating anything then.

She had loved to eat ever since her childhood and now she wasn't able to do even that.

Neither her Shivji, nor Sankat Mochan were listening to my prayers. Whose door was I to knock to save my precious Ma's life?

The doctor came up to me and Rahul and said, 'Next few hours are critical.'

His voice seemed as if it came from a distance. I had gone numb. My friends had taken me away to make me eat, I think, but I came back to sit with Ma. Rahul let me. The staff also let me. Last few hours . . .

I pulled up a chair.

And sat next to her.

She lay peacefully.

No pain on her face now.

She was glowing in fact.

'How will I survive without you, Ma?'

And then I started chatting with her, singing her favourite 1950s songs, reciting her poems, absorbing that moment . . .

I tightened the grip of her hand in my hand . . .

I kept my head on her hand.

The one who gave me unconditional love . . .

My best friend . . .

My little daughter now . . .

What a wonderful life she had given me! What a wonderful mother she had been to us! And what a woman!

I sat there looking at her . . .

Till the doctor signalled to me that it was over . . .

No, it wasn't over for me . . .

I had and always will hold her hand.

She walks with me step by step, showing herself in the purple hues everywhere, smiling at me . . .

I sit here reminiscing about my moments with this magnificent lady who I was extremely fortunate to have as my Ma and my baby . . .

27

Picking Up the Pieces of My Life

§

As I put on my '*besan ka lep*' (face pack), tears roll down my face . . . Ma used to run after me saying, '*Dekh laga le, sunder lagegi. Main nai houngi na, to koi ni poochega* (Put this on, it will make you more beautiful. When I am no longer around, nobody will ask after you like this).' She would also pop a few multivitamins in my mouth murmuring, '*Actress hain bhai, sunder dikhna teri duty hai* (Since you are an actress, it is your duty to look beautiful).'

Her voice still resounds in my ears as I put her pack on my face and pop those multivitamins. Yes, no one's asked me to since she left. But had she been around, she would have. And she is around.

I am trying to make peace with this thought.

I started with denial . . . living normally, giving everyone else strength, thinking Ma had passed on all her strength to me. And I had become like her. But like J.P. Dutta and Sonu Nigam had warned me, it hits you later . . . each moment spent, things done together, the absence.

It hits me now. I suddenly turn towards her side of the bed to discuss the day's happenings with my roommate and I realize she's not there. I eat back my words . . . with tears trickling out of my eyes, I look for her desperately. The heart yearns to see her . . .

Initially, I started with putting her newspaper and specs on the bed like she used to when I was home with her. And I would make her black tea with elaichi in her steel tumbler and keep it by her bedside. And hug her clothes. That's the closest I could get to her physically . . . the sheer helplessness of the situation made me howl endlessly till I got tired of crying. Coming back home reminded me of her. Everything. The room, the kitchen, the chair where she sat smiling, looking outside the window . . .

Ma was also very smart. She wanted to help me deal with such a situation. In my twenty-year-long career, I have never been away from home for seven to eight months continuously. I made sure I would come home in short breaks in between to meet her. But after she passed away, I started having to go for longer shoots and I have a feeling that she is behind this plan, so I can learn to deal with her absence away from home. Meet people, be busy.

I am sharing this with you all today without any awkwardness or embarrassment. Even at work, I would give a super shot and come back to the vanity van and cry. The habit of calling up Ma after I would reach the shoot would tear me apart . . . How would I hear her voice ever again? Those reassuringly lively words! That word, 'beta' . . . That laughter.

I tried hard to not ruin my mascara, but the tears flowed and I howled. Yes, I howled in my vanity van. I still do. There is an urge sometimes to look for her like I would in my childhood while playing blind man's bluff and out of nowhere I would catch hold of Ma. I wish I could pull her out of somewhere and say, 'Caught you!'

I would start chatting randomly with her, hoping and wishing she was hearing me. But I wanted to hear her too.

My desperation for wanting Ma was getting me angry now . . . And I was getting irritable about every little thing . . .

The migraines had turned worse . . . And Rahul finally asked me to go to a psychiatrist.

It was during those days that I read about Deepika Padukone writing about her depression and working simultaneously. I was doing the same, I thought. It is strange how you live life on two different levels. One for the world and one for yourself.

The doctor I consulted said I was in a state of trauma which led to the severe headaches. My medicine pouch was growing bigger every day, even more than my mother's. I used to once make fun of *Ma ki dawaiyon ka dabba* (Ma's medicine box). '*Ma kitni dawaiyan khati ho, yaar* (How many medicines you have, Ma)!' I would tell her.

I popped a pill to soothe my nerves. I had to look normal for my shot. And smiling. And strong. Strangely, it magically happened.

I guess when I was with people I could still deal with my trauma, distract myself. It was being in my own company that was the hazard. My head would fill up with a zillion thoughts. Of denial, disbelief, helplessness, sadness and anger. It was work, work and work and there was me. In totality, a lot to deal with.

Friends have been so kind. Giving me an ear whenever I needed them. I am lucky Ma gave me a brother as loving as Rahul, who cares for me like a father and loves me so much. He has been the stronger one and he understands my journey has been tough. He has seen me break down in between a normal conversation. He has made me sit on his lap and mothered me too. He is trying to help me find Ma in him but he already is Ma's best gift to me.

I have a very affectionate family in my two bachchas, my little pet, Sakhi, and my nephew, Vehaant. They are my lifeline. So much unconditional love pours out from them. When I come home, the way they both jump on me to cuddle me, I feel am getting familiar with happiness once again.

And my super caring bhabhi ... she's a younger sister one would want to come home to and share one's day's events with. I am fortunate. Yes. But still the journey's mine alone ...

I still feel the vacuum left by my best friend ...

In the airplane seat next to me, in the bedroom next to me ... at my special occasions next to me. I miss loving her. Doing things for her. Pampering her.

But she's doing it again now. She is making me stand up on my two feet again.

She met me finally . . . in my dream . . . And I cried and cried and did all the *shikayat*s (complaints) that I had in my heart . . . she was quiet . . . all she said was, 'Not being there doesn't mean I am not close to you . . . Bas.'

They say you get messages through songs. In the morning the first song that played in my car was, '*Tu jahan jahan rahega mera saya sath hoga . . . tu agar udas hoga to udas hongi mai bhi . . . nazar aaon ya na aaon, tere paas hongi main bhi* (Whether you can see me or not, I will always be by your side . . . your sadness will sadden me).'

She had said what she had to. Made her point as always.

I am now trying to pick up the pieces of my life again.

Like you all think I am strong, that belief was put in my head by my mother, I realize that now. Because I can still hear it in my head that I can do it. I can make it.

So the first step has been taken. The dawaiyon ka dabba has been thrown out.

When I miss Ma, I look for her in people and try doing little things . . . Like this old aunty I saw at the airport the other day. She so reminded me of Ma. She was looking for some assistance and I literally jumped and gave her a helping hand. She hugged me and smiled. I could feel Ma looking at us and smiling. She likes it when I do these things. And she replies to me in all things purple because purple was her favourite colour. In fact my friend, Rajit Kapur, nicknamed her 'Purple'!

I was walking on the beach the other day and met two friends of Ma. Instantly, I missed the third member of that group. My heart skipped a beat and there was a lump in my throat. But something told me I shouldn't cry. Then the waves touched my feet. Also, a small purple shell stuck to the corner of my foot . . . yeah, she was there . . .

She tells me I need to move on. She gives me signs. I still need to be her strong girl and make her proud always. There is nothing better than being called *Nalini ki beti*!

28

Of Ice Creams and More

§

I feel Ma talk to me when I really need advice . . . yes, like an inner voice. She lives on within and she guides me when I am feeling lost.

I remember, as a schoolgirl, I had once come home crying . . . with two melted ice creams in my hands. I hadn't even touched them. Ma became worried and asked me what happened, why I had come in that state from school. I was inconsolable. 'What happened?', she asked again. In between all the crying, I could barely speak. *Ma, Romi ne ice cream nai khayi* (Ma, Romi did not eat the ice cream).'

Ma was confused. I continued, 'Ma, I bought an ice cream for Romi and she refused! She did not reciprocate my friendship.'

And I howled again.

Romi was my schoolmate. We used to travel in the same school van. We never really got along until I decided one day to mend bridges and initiate a step towards friendship. But she had refused. I was hurt. Very hurt. My good gesture was turned down! I couldn't digest it.

Ma made me sit on her lap and tried to calm me down. Then she sweetly called Romi's mother and shared with her what had happened. She had to explain to me as well. She turned towards me. 'Romi didn't have your ice cream. But in the process you didn't have yours either!'

I looked at the wasted melted ice creams. Yes, I could have enjoyed my share of my favourite ice cream at least. But I was too busy sweating over another person not having it.

That was years back . . .

But Ma always kept telling me over time to do what I could do best and leave it at that.

Other people's actions would impact me. It would bother me that sometimes people were not nice to me when I was pleasant to them. But she explained to me that if I held on to the hurt, in the process I would end up hurting myself more. I should not waste time thinking about other people's opinions.

Some things remain unchanged. Recently, I was walking on the beach, upset with someone for not reciprocating my friendly gesture and feeling helpless about it when a whiff of fresh air blew on my face and I could hear Ma talk to me smilingly, 'Romi didn't have your ice cream again?'

It got me thinking. This had to change. I got some perspective immediately.

As I think of resolutions at the beginning of a new year, I promise myself not to be bothered by other people's actions and reactions, to not let my happiness depend on outside factors. I promise to make best friends with myself, to pamper myself with that ice cream that I allowed to melt in my hand for so many years and forgot to enjoy. My job is to do what is right. It is not in my hands or my job to bother about other people's reactions to it. If someone doesn't take the ice cream, too bad. I shall have both, I promise myself . . . this time with a smile on my face.

And yes, I can sense Ma smiling too.

I promise myself I'll smile and be happy because that's how she'd like me to be.

So here's to new beginnings, new hopes and dreams and lots of delicious ice creams!

Epilogue

〜

So my dearest readers, I am holding Ma's hand still, the little child in me intact. And moving on in the direction she shows. As I wrap four beautiful films up and get an applause from my crew, I know she sits in the corner on her chair and smiles . . . As I wrap up this book to share this amazing journey with my Nalini, with you, I am sure she's very happy because she knows you all mean a lot to me . . .

And to you Ma, just a big thank you, Gudiya, for being who you were in my life. And the love you gave me.

How many can feel this completeness that I experienced in one life? The love that she gave me . . . even if I share it with millions, there will be a lot more tucked away in my heart.

As for me . . .

Ma, I wait here, doing my job as well as you would want me to, talking to you every day about the silly things I do, having my chai with you in your steel tumbler, finding you in all things purple, smiling at me, wishing you 'good morning' and 'good night'. Loving you and fighting with you.

All this and more until I meet you on the other side.

To write another beautiful story . . .

Together.

Acknowledgements

～

As I sit to pen down a few acknowledgements, the first name that comes to mind is my brother's, Dr Rahul Dutta. We have always been the best of friends, but after Ma he became a parent to me—loving, caring and protective. I took his help with hypnotherapy too, to find myself again. Those sessions helped me regain my positivity. Rahul has been the first person to have heard all that I finally got down to writing and to have given the most honest feedback that I could count on. His opinion mattered; after all, this book is about the two most special women in his life! Thanks bhaiya (as I fondly call my younger brother). This book wouldn't be possible without your soothing presence in my life and your strong hand on my shoulder.

Thank you my sweet and simple bhabhi, Shweta! You have smiled and cried listening to all the chapters in this book. Your emotional responses have reassured me that I was doing something right.

Thanks to my bachchas, Vehaant and Sakhi, who gave me all the smiles and rejuvenating energy to give this book my sincerest best.

Thank you my dear 2-a.m. friends, you know who you all are—Jyotica (my cousin), Sonu Nigam, Rajit, Archana, Richa, Radhika, Sunnaeya, Monika, Sanjay, Ruxana, Tariq, Vikas, Asheesh—for helping me sail through this tough one year, for making sure I didn't lose focus because of my lows, for hearing me out patiently, and reading my chapters and remembering Ma with me.

Thank you my dear directors, Neeraj Pandey, Sriram Raghwan, Rakesh Mehra, for guiding me on how to go about my first book, when all I had was intent and a story to tell.

Thank you so much, Shabana Azmi! Apart from being someone I have idolized, you, in all these years have become a strong pillar of strength for me. You stood by me through Ma's illness and after her, like a rock. And a huge thank you for the beautiful foreword. I couldn't have thought of anyone else to write it but you . . . *shukriya*.

And finally, thanks Ma! My inspiration. I remember I sat in the ICU, seeing you and randomly these words came to my mind, 'Me and Ma . . .' what a journey with you . . . so much to tell and share about you . . . so much to share about a complete bond between a mother and a daughter who also happened to be best friends . . . thanks for being you. This story is yours. And I, an integral part of a beautiful journey with you . . .